Pat Halverson

Tense Drills

L. W. Giggins/D. J. Shoebridge

TENSE DRILLS

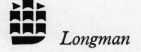 *Longman*

LONGMAN GROUP LIMITED
Longman House
Burnt Mill, Harlow, Essex.

© Longman Group Ltd 1970

First published 1970
New impressions *1970; *1971;
*1973; *1975; *1976; *1977 ;
*1979; *1981

ISBN 0 582 52173 4

Printed in Hong Kong by
Wing Tai Cheung Printing Co Ltd

Contents

THE PAST CONTINUOUS

THE PRESENT PERFECT SIMPLE

THE PAST PERFECT CONTINUOUS

Introduction

The teacher of English as a second or foreign language is usually well aware that an oral approach to learning is the best one, yet he is not uncommonly in a position where suitable oral material is difficult to come by. Oral work has to be controlled and disciplined, and each particular point has to be pressed home by frequent drilling. It is the aim of this book to provide such oral material for systematic practice in the use of the tenses.

How to use the book

ARRANGEMENT

For convenience, the tenses are dealt with in a conventional sequence (Present, Past, Future) and are graded Elementary, Intermediate or Advanced. This grading indicates the level at which the particular use may be introduced, though many units marked Elementary may profitably be used with Intermediate students and those marked Intermediate (or even Elementary) with Advanced students for revision or remedial purposes.

METHOD

From the above, it will be understood that the book is not intended to be worked through unit by unit, nor even that the units marked Elementary or those marked Intermediate should be worked through in order. For example, all the drills on the Past Perfect Simple are marked Intermediate, yet it is not necessary or desirable to practise them consecutively in one group. Certain tenses or uses of tenses may usefully be compared and practised in conjunction with others; where this involves two separate units in this book (e.g. Units 18 and 26), a note in one unit refers the teacher to the other so that they may be practised together.

To a certain extent, the teacher may find it desirable to adapt sentences to suit his class; bracketed words and alternatives within a sentence are intended to show where this may be necessary. If, for example, the book is being used outside England, it is clearly unsuitable to ask 'When did you come to England?' (Unit 16, Section A); the word *England* may be substituted by any other suitable name of a country or place. Similarly in Unit 7, the choice between *shirt/blouse* will depend on whether the question is directed at a male or female student; if the female student happens to be wearing a dress, the teacher should further adapt the question. The aim must be to make all questions directed at students as realistic as possible.

While the teacher is free to use these drills in the way that best suits the needs of his students, it is nevertheless important that he should follow closely the Method set out at the head of the units. In units where there is no Method given, the drills are straightforward and the Example is sufficient to show how they should be done. The teacher should insist on accuracy in the students' responses, but at the same time these must be as fluent and natural as possible. The responses in certain drills depend for their full effect on correct stress and intonation, and the students will often need help from the teacher in this respect. In some cases, where stress is of great importance for the correct understanding of the response, a note concerning this has been included before the drill. It is also important that the students should know what they are practising and why, and the teacher should always explain the Aim of the unit (with reference to the Example) before beginning it.

TYPES OF DRILL

The drills are of different types: Question and Answer, Conversion and Completion. Quite apart from the necessity to practise certain things in certain ways, it is hoped that this will provide variety. It will also be noticed that different drills aim to practise different aspects of a tense. For some of the tenses there are initial drills consisting of questions and answers relating to actions performed in the classroom; the purpose of these is to demonstrate more clearly the fundamental use and meaning of a particular tense. Other drills aim to practise the forms of a tense (e.g. Question and Negative forms) or the pronunciation of particular forms (e.g. the 3rd Person singular -*s*, -*es*, or the -*d*, -*ed* of the Past Tense). Very often tense usage is closely related to particular sentence structures; consequently there are drills to practise the use of a tense with different conjunctions and adverbs (e.g. the Past Continuous with *just as*; the Present Perfect with *yet*, *still*, *ever/never*, etc.; the Past Perfect with *until*, *already*, *no sooner*.

CUES

Wherever possible, drills should be done without the students looking at their books. In a number of units cues are provided and for these books may be used; however, as soon as the students have become familiar with the form of the drill and the responses required, the drill should be repeated with books closed, the teacher prompting with cues only when a student needs help. In some cases Advanced students may like to make their own responses; this should be encouraged whenever possible (e.g. Unit 63).

In cases where the students have no books, the cues may be used in various other ways. Teachers may wish to make tapes for these drills for use with a recorder or in a language laboratory. Alternatively, the cues may be written on the blackboard before practice begins, or the teacher may call out each cue after he has given the stimulus. With some of the drills, when the cue consists of a single word or short phrase (e.g. Units 64 and 69), the cues should be called out by the teacher whether the students have books or not.

WRITTEN WORK

Many of the drills provide suitable material for written work. When a drill has been practised orally (more than once if necessary), it may be given for written practice in class or as homework.

Perhaps a general word may be said here about drilling. It sounds so dull and impersonal. It need not be at all. If students understand the purpose and value of it, and see how, by its *varied repetition*, it assists them to produce correct structures as well as to grasp more clearly the functions of a tense, they will become enthusiastic for something that should, after all, be one of their main aims: accuracy and fluency in speaking English. Much depends on the teacher: if he finds the whole process boring, who can blame the students if they do too? If the teacher is fired with zeal for his task, then they may catch his enthusiasm.

THE PRESENT CONTINUOUS

To present or revise the PRESENT CONTINUOUS *used for*

actions in the REAL PRESENT.

Method Each group of actions should be taken separately as set out below. When the first group has been acted and repeated, the same method is followed with the second group, and so on.

The teacher does each action in the group and during each action he says what he is doing. He then repeats these actions, asking the students what he is doing. The students reply as in the example. The teacher should take care that the action is continued or repeated until the response has been made.

Example

TEACHER: (while walking to the window) I'm walking to the window.
(while looking out of the window) I'm looking out of the window. etc.

TEACHER: (while walking to the window) What am I doing?
STUDENT: You're walking to the window.
TEACHER: (while looking out of the window) What am I doing?
STUDENT: You're looking out of the window. etc.

● *Drill*

He walks to the window.
  looks out of the window.
  opens the window.
  closes the window.
  walks back to the desk.

He looks at Mr X.
  points to Miss Y.
  smiles at Mr Z.
  carries a chair.
  drinks water.

He knocks on the desk.
  winds his watch.
  bends down.
  pulls up his socks.
  ties his shoelace.

He cuts a piece of paper.
  holds up his hand.
  draws on the blackboard.
  cries.
  laughs.

He reads a book.
  turns over the pages of the book.
  writes on the blackboard.
  wipes the blackboard.
  jumps up and down.

If the drill is being used for revision purposes, more advanced vocabulary may be introduced.

He scratches his head.	He brushes his jacket.
coughs.	shakes hands with Mr Y.
blows his nose.	waves his handkerchief.
yawns.	leans against the wall.
stretches.	folds/tears a piece of paper. etc.

UNIT **2**   *Elementary*

To practise the PRESENT CONTINUOUS (*affirmative and*

negative) *for actions in the* REAL PRESENT.

Note   The teacher should insist on the correct contractions throughout the drill. In particular, students should use the form *he/she isn't* instead of the form *he/she's not*. (Although the latter would be correct, it is less usual.)

Example

TEACHER TO STUDENT A:	Stand on your right leg.
TEACHER TO STUDENT B:	Ask him if he's standing on his left leg.
STUDENT B:	Are you standing on your left leg?
STUDENT A:	No, I'm not.
*TEACHER TO STUDENT B:	What does he say?
STUDENT B:	He says he isn't standing on his left leg.
TEACHER TO STUDENT B:	Ask him what he's doing.
STUDENT B:	What are you doing?
STUDENT A:	I'm standing on my right leg.
*TEACHER TO STUDENT B:	What does he say?
STUDENT B:	He says he's standing on his right leg.
TEACHER TO STUDENT B:	Is he standing on his left leg?
STUDENT B:	No, he isn't.

*It should be possible to leave out 'What does he say?' after a few examples.

●*Drill*

sitting on the table:	sitting on a chair.
writing with his right hand:	writing with his left hand.
pointing to a window:	pointing to the door.
writing with a blue pen:	writing with a red pen.
holding up his right hand:	holding up his left hand.
looking at Mr X:	looking at Miss Y.

reading from a green book:	reading from a blue book.
shaking hands with Mr Y:	shaking hands with Mr Z.
eating a sweet:	eating a biscuit.
drawing a house (on the blackboard):	drawing a ship.
cutting the paper with scissors:	cutting the paper with a knife.
scratching his head:	scratching his back.
tapping the desk:	tapping the wall.
leaning against the wall:	leaning on the desk.
holding the book in his right hand:	holding the book in his left hand.
wiping the blackboard:	wiping the window.
cleaning his glasses:	cleaning his shoes.
kneeling on the chair:	kneeling on the floor.
carrying a handbag:	carrying a book.

UNIT 3   *Elementary and Intermediate*

To practise the REAL PRESENT *with less demonstrable ideas, and with a variety of subjects.*

Example

TEACHER TO STUDENT A:	Ask him if he's listening to the teacher.
STUDENT A TO STUDENT B:	Are you listening to the teacher?
STUDENT B:	Yes, I am.
(or)	No, I'm not.
TEACHER TO STUDENT A:	What does he say?
STUDENT A:	He says he's listening to the teacher.
(or)	He says he isn't listening to the teacher.

●*Drill*

Are you enjoying your English classes?
Are you living at home?
Are you paying attention?
Are you sitting comfortably?
Are you trying hard?
Are you learning a lot of English?
Are you feeling hot/cold?
Are you sitting in your usual place?
Are you looking forward to the holidays?
Are you longing for the weekend?
Are you sitting next to your friend?
Are you thinking about (France, Persia, your sister, etc.)?
Are you wearing a clean (shirt, blouse, etc.)?
Are you attending to the lesson?
Are you carrying a comb in your pocket?

The teacher should explain that in the following examples there will be a variety of subjects.

> Are we doing an easy exercise?
> Are they coming here?
> Is Peter living in (London) at present?
> Are they studying English at present?
> Is she waiting for him?
> Are we working hard?
> Am I speaking clearly enough?
> Are they attending school?
> Is David taking an exam now?
> Are they travelling down from (London)?
> Am I talking properly?
> Is Susan cooking your lunch at the moment?
> Are they wearing hats?
> Is Philip behaving well?
> Are we practising well?
> Are they expecting a letter?

UNIT 4   *Advanced*

To practise the special use of the PRESENT CONTINUOUS

with always.

Note The Present Continuous is sometimes used with *always* (more rarely with *continually*, *for ever*) to emphasise the frequency with which an action is repeated: the speaker wishes to show that, in his opinion, this action occurs more frequently than is normal, and the feeling conveyed is usually one of surprise, irritation or criticism. Look at the following examples:

(a) I'*m always seeing* him on the bus. (suggesting surprise)
(b) She'*s always changing* her mind. (suggesting irritation)
(c) He'*s always going* to the doctor with some small complaint. (criticism—it's nothing to do with me how often he goes, but he's wasting the doctor's valuable time)
(d) They're a very friendly people and *are always smiling*. (statement of fact)

However, people's reactions to what happens vary, and circumstances also may affect our reactions; it is therefore important in this drill that each student should decide for himself which feeling he wishes to convey and that he should try to convey this by correct intonation. Notice that there should always be a stress on *always*, the heavier the stress the greater the feeling of surprise or irritation. (See Unit 34, p. 51, for the use of *always* with the Past Continuous.)

Example
TEACHER: He teases the dog very, very often.
STUDENT: He's always teasing the dog.

● *Drill*
He plays the piano all the time.
He makes mistakes all the time.
She has accidents very, very often.
He argues with me all the time.
He goes to the pictures too much.
She has parties very, very often.
She tells me about her family all the time.
You forget to bring your book very, very often.
He smiles all the time.
She loses her glasses very often.
He complains about his work too much.
She buys new clothes very, very often
She goes up to (London) very, very often.
He talks about television programmes too much.
She asks for advice very often.
He makes silly remarks all the time.
He borrows money too often.
She talks about her neighbours too much.
He makes trouble all the time.
She tells us how clever her husband is too often.
Our radio goes wrong all the time.
She interferes with things all the time.
This clock stops nearly every day.
She ladders her stockings all the time.
He boasts about his garden all the time.
Our car breaks down very often.
She grumbles about her health all the time.
This zip comes undone all the time.
She has her hair done too often.
This pen runs out all the time.
He bites his nails all the time.
She rings me up very, very often.
This necklace breaks very often.
He comes home after midnight too often.
She criticises me all the time.

THE SIMPLE PRESENT

To present or revise the HABITUAL PRESENT *and practise*

the form of the tense.

Example

*Stage One

TEACHER TO STUDENT A:	How many cups of coffee do you drink every day?
STUDENT A:	I drink . . . cups of coffee every day.

Stage Two

TEACHER TO STUDENT B:	Ask A how many cups of coffee he drinks every day.
STUDENT B TO STUDENT A:	How many cups of coffee do you drink every day?
STUDENT A:	I drink . . . cups of coffee every day.
*TEACHER TO STUDENT B:	What does he say?
STUDENT B:	He says he drinks . . . cups of coffee every day.

Stage Three

TEACHER TO STUDENT B:	Ask him if he drinks (different number) cups of coffee every day.
STUDENT B TO STUDENT A:	Do you drink (different number) cups of coffee every day?
STUDENT A:	No, I don't.
*TEACHER TO STUDENT B:	What does he say?
STUDENT B:	He says he doesn't drink (different number) cups of coffee every day.

*It should be possible to omit these parts after a few examples.

●*Drill*

How many times do you go to the cinema every month?
How many meals do you eat every day?
How many letters do you write every month?
How many hours do you spend in school every day?
How many times do you have your hair cut every month?
How many times do you clean your teeth every day?
How often do you wash your hair every month?
How long do you work every day?
How many days do you attend school every week?
How do you come to school?

How long do you sit in the classroom every day?
How often do you listen to the radio?
How much money do you get every week?
How much time do you spend on your homework?
How do you treat your brother/sister?

What do you write your homework with?
What do you have for breakfast?
What do you carry your books in?
What do you bring to school with you?
What do you clean your teeth with?
What game do you play?
What bus do you get to school?
What languages do you speak?
What colour shoes do you wear for school?
What sort of restaurant do you go to?
What kind of records do you buy?
What kind of books do you read?

What time do you get up?
What time do you have breakfast?
What time do you leave for school?
What time do you arrive at school?
What time do you stop for coffee?
What time do you eat lunch?
What time do you have tea?
What time do you begin your homework?
What time do you have dinner?
What time do you go to bed?

Where do you have breakfast?
Where do you listen to records?
Where do you hang your clothes?
Where do you have your English lessons?
Where do you drive your car fast?
Where do you meet your friends?
Where do you swim?
Where do you keep your books?
Where do you go for your holidays?
Where do you keep your money?

In the following examples the teacher should ensure that the students make their answers with an adverbial of time and NOT with a *when*-clause. It may be necessary to prompt the students in some answers. Some suggestions for this are given in brackets after the questions.

When do you go for your holidays?   (in the summer/in the winter)
When do you wear thick clothes?   (in the winter/in the summer)
When do you do your homework?   (in the evening/in the afternoon)
When do you go out dancing?   (at the weekend/during the week)

When do you feel tired?	(in the evening/in the morning)
When do you receive presents?	(on my birthday/every day)
When do you feel thirsty?	(on a hot day/on a cold day)
When do you work very hard?	(before an exam/in the holidays)˙
When do you sit near the fire?	(on cold days/on hot days)
When do you look at television?	(in the evenings/in the mornings)

With a class that has thoroughly grasped the procedure of the drill, it should be possible to practise the last three sections with call-words only.

Èxample

TEACHER TO STUDENT A:	wake up
STUDENT A TO STUDENT B:	What time do you wake up?
STUDENT B:	I wake up at seven o'clock.
STUDENT A:	He says he wakes up at seven o'clock.
TEACHER TO STUDENT A:	half past eight
STUDENT A TO STUDENT B:	Do you wake up at half past eight?
STUDENT B:	No, I don't.
STUDENT A:	He says he doesn't wake up at half past eight.

UNIT 6 *Elementary*

To practise the 3RD PERSON SINGULAR ENDINGS *when pronounced* /s/ *or* /z/ (*PART I*), *and when pronounced* /iz/ (*PART II*).

Method The teacher provides the stimulus, and the students repeat this, continuing with a contrasting idea about 'my brother/sister/cousin', etc.

Part I pronounced /s/ or /z/

Examples
TEACHER: I speak English well . . .
STUDENT: I speak English well but my brother speaks English badly.

TEACHER: I keep a cat . . .
STUDENT: I keep a cat but my cousin keeps a dog.

TEACHER: I grow tomatoes in my.garden . . .
STUDENT: I grow tomatoes in my garden but my sister grows flowers (in her garden).

●*Drill*

I like coffee but my brother . . .
I walk slowly but my sister . . .
I get up early but my aunt . . .
I drink tea . . .
I eat three times a day . . .
I listen to classical music . . .
I go to bed at ten o'clock . . .
I have lunch at one o'clock . . .
I wear a grey suit . . .
I prefer fair-haired girls . . .
I collect records . . .
I wake up at half past seven . . .
I play the violin . . .
I live in (Brighton) . . .
I talk quietly . . .
I want a radio . . .
I understand three languages . . .
I spend my holidays in (France) . . .
I come to school in the morning . . .
I do my work well . . .
I ride a horse . . .
I buy expensive clothes . . .
I write letters on Saturdays . . .
I look young . . .
I start work at eight o'clock . . .
I open my letters before breakfast . . .
I see one film every week . . .
I study in the afternoon . . .
I travel by car . . .
I visit my friends on Saturday . . .
I take ten minutes to get to school . . .
I lay the table for breakfast . . .
I leave home at eight o'clock . . .

Part II pronounced /iz/

Example
TEACHER: I catch a No 27 bus . . .
STUDENT: I catch a No 27 bus but my brother catches a No 19 bus.

●*Drill*

I finish work at six o'clock but my sister . . .
I teach English but my uncle . . .
I use my car at weekends but my brother . . .
I catch an early train . . .
I brush my teeth in the morning . . .
I watch television twice a week . . .
I fetch the children at four o'clock . . .

I pass the Post Office on my way to work . . .
I lose my umbrella about once a month . . .
I wash my hands before lunch . . .
I practise the piano three hours a day . . .
I close the shop at five o'clock . . .
I manage a restaurant . . .
I dance till ten o'clock . . .
I reach work at nine o'clock . . .
I dress well . . .
I arrange books carelessly . . .
I cross the road at the traffic-lights . . .
I crash my car about once a year . . .
I cash my cheque on Fridays . . .

UNIT 7   *Elementary*

To practise the 3RD PERSON SINGULAR ENDING *when*

pronounced /iz/.

Method   As for Stage 2 of Unit 5.

Example

TEACHER TO STUDENT A:	Ask B when he closes the shop.
STUDENT A TO STUDENT B:	When do you close the shop?
STUDENT B:	I close the shop at half past five.
*TEACHER TO STUDENT A:	What does he say?
STUDENT A:	He says he closes the shop at half past five.

*It should be possible to omit 'What does he say?' after a few examples.

● *Drill*
What time do you finish work?
When do you use your car?
When do you brush your teeth?
How often do you watch television?
What time do you reach school?
Where do you cross the road?
What time do you fetch the children?
What drink do you prefer?
How often do you change your shirt/blouse?
When do you arrange your holidays?
When do you wash?
Where do you dress?
What bus do you catch to school?
When do you refuse to get up early?

UNIT **8**   *Elementary*

To practise the 3RD PERSON, *singular and plural, with noun subjects.*

Examples

TEACHER: A barber cuts hair.
STUDENT: A barber cuts hair.
Barbers cut hair.

TEACHER: Cats like milk.
STUDENT: Cats like milk.
A cat likes milk.

●*Drill*
A dog barks.
A butcher sells meat.
Tailors make clothes.
A gardener grows flowers.
Bears like honey.
An encyclopedia gives information.
Birds fly.
A clock ticks.
Monkeys eat bananas.
Fish swim.
A cat likes fish.
Pilots fly aeroplanes.
A cow gives milk.
A refrigerator keeps food cool.
A nurse looks after sick people.
Wasps sting.
Bees make honey.
A chicken lays eggs.
Trains travel on rails.
A secretary types letters.

UNIT **9**	*Elementary and Intermediate*

To practise the 3RD PERSON SINGULAR *(ending in /s/ or /z/).*

SECTION A

In this section the students answer each question using the verb suggested by the noun in the question.

Example.
TEACHER: What does a skater do?
STUDENT: He/She skates.

●*Drill*

What does a singer do?
What does an actor do?
What does a runner do?
What does a cook do?
What does a diver do?
What does a lecturer do?
What does a gardener do?
What does a writer do?
What does a painter do?
What does a builder do?

What does a climber do?
What does a smoker do?
What does a driver do?
What does a swimmer do?
What does a conductor do?
What does a bather do?
What does a typist do?
What does a worker do?
What does a traveller do?
What does a cyclist do?

SECTION B

In this section students may use any obvious verb, provided the ending has the sound /s/ or /z/.

Example
TEACHER: What does a dog do?
STUDENT: It barks.

●*Drill*

What does a bird do?
What does a fish do?
What does a thief do?
What does a bell do?
What does a fire do?

What does a baby do?
What does a knife do?
What does a student do?
What does the sun do?
What does the wind do?

In sections C and D, the teacher may use the verb suggested in brackets to prompt the student when the drill is first attempted, or in case of difficulty.

SECTION C

In this section, the student supplies suitable verbs and objects.

Example
TEACHER: What does a violinist do?   (play)
STUDENT: He plays the violin.

●*Drill*

What does a baker do?	(sell)
What does a photographer do?	(take)
What does a pianist do?	(play)
What does a barber do?	(cut)
What does a grocer do?	(sell)
What does a tailor do?	(make)
What does a stamp-collector do?	(collect)
What does a shoe-repairer do?	(mend)
What does a postman do?	(deliver)
What does a footballer do?	(play)
What does a salesman do?	(sell)
What does a dentist do?	(pull out)
What does an optician do?	(test)
What does an architect do?	(design)
What does a carpenter do?	(make)
What does a florist do?	(sell)
What does a pilot do?	(fly)
What does a waiter do?	(serve)

SECTION D

This section is intended for more advanced students.

Example
TEACHER: What does an encyclopedia do?   (give)
STUDENT: It gives information.

●*Drill*

What does a gramophone do?	(play)
What does an oven do?	(cook)
What does a lift do?	(take)
What does a refrigerator do?	(keep)
What does a clock do?	(tell)
What does an electric kettle do?	(boil)
What does a lawn-mower do?	(cut)
What does a lorry do?	(carry)
What does a newspaper do?	(give)
What does a calendar do?	(tell)

UNIT **10**   *Elementary*

To practise DOES *in short-form answers.*

Note   The teacher should make sure that the students stress only the noun in their answers.

Example
TEACHER: Who acts?
STUDENT: An actor does.

> ●*Drill*
> Who bakes bread?
> Who mends shoes?
> Who conducts an orchestra?
> Who repairs watches?
> Who makes furniture?
> Who sells vegetables?
> Who writes books?
> Who paints pictures?
> Who plays the piano?
> Who makes men's suits?
> Who cuts men's hair?
> Who delivers letters?
> Who sells medicine?
> Who serves food in a restaurant?
> Who carries luggage at a station?
> Who controls traffic?
> Who designs buildings?
> Who flies aeroplanes?
> Who takes photographs?
> Who pulls out teeth?

UNIT **11**   *Elementary*

To practise DOES *and* DOESN'T *in short-form answers.*

Examples

TEACHER TO STUDENT A:	Ask him if he likes chocolates.
STUDENT A TO STUDENT B:	Do you like chocolates?
STUDENT B:	Yes, I do.
*TEACHER TO STUDENT A:	What does he say?
STUDENT A:	He says he likes chocolates.
TEACHER TO STUDENT A:	Does he like chocolates?
STUDENT A:	Yes, he does.
TEACHER TO STUDENT A:	Ask him if he smokes.
STUDENT A TO STUDENT B:	Do you smoke?
STUDENT B:	No, I don't.
*TEACHER TO STUDENT A:	What does he say?
STUDENT A:	He says he doesn't smoke.
TEACHER TO STUDENT A:	Does he smoke?
STUDENT A:	No, he doesn't.

*It should be possible to leave out 'What does he say?' after a few examples.

●*Drill*

Do you like classical music?
Do you walk to school?
Do you drink whisky?
Do you come here every day?
Do you go to the cinema at the weekend?
Do you travel by train every day?
Do you cycle to school?
Do you spend your holidays in (France)?
Do you take sugar in your tea?
Do you drive a car?
Do you stay out late?
Do you eat a lot?
Do you sleep well?
Do you listen to the radio a lot?
Do you have lessons on Saturday?

UNIT 12   *Intermediate*

To practise verbs that are NOT USUALLY FOUND IN THE CONTINUOUS PRESENT.

Note   There are a number of verbs which are rarely or never used in the continuous tenses, even when the reference is clearly to the Real Present. These are mainly verbs that refer to conditions or types of behaviour that are not fully under human control.

They include:

(a) VERBS OF PERCEPTION, such as *see, hear, notice,* etc., which refer to the receiving of knowledge through the senses. Since we have eyes, we see; since we have ears, we hear; but we cannot decide what to see or what to hear (though we can decide what to look at, and what to listen to.)

(b) NON-CONCLUSIVE VERBS, which refer to: Mental States, such as *know, understand, mean,* etc.; Emotional States, such as *like, want, mind,* etc.; Circumstantial States, referring to things as they are, such as *contain, belong, need,* etc. The common characteristic of these notions is that they are involuntary, that is, they cannot be begun or ended at will. We can choose to learn something or not, but we cannot choose to know something; we can choose to eat an apple or not, but we cannot choose to like apples; we can choose to buy or sell something, but we cannot choose to need it.

It should, however, be noted that some of these verbs may be found in the continuous forms:

(a) for special emphasis, e.g. (I can hear a noise). You're *always hearing* noises.

(b) when the verb is used in another sense, e.g. She's *minding* the baby (She's minding = She's looking after).

Example

TEACHER TO STUDENT A:	Ask him if he remembers the telephone number.
STUDENT A TO STUDENT B:	Do you remember the telephone number?
STUDENT B:	Yes, I do.
	(or) No, I don't.
*TEACHER TO STUDENT A:	What does he say?
STUDENT A:	He says he remembers the telephone number.
	He says he doesn't remember the telephone number.

*It should be possible to leave out 'What does he say?' after a few examples.

●*Drill*
Do you hear a noise?
Do you agree with me?
Do you see that mark on the wall?
Do you think his answer's right?
Do you believe the story?
Do you smell gas?
Do you know the answer?
Do you remember her name?
Do you understand the lesson?
Do you see what I mean?
Do you recognise that boy over there?
Do you trust him?
Do you suppose he'll come?
Do you realise your mistake?
Do you like this book?
Do you want another one?
Do you dislike rain?
Do you mind waiting for a minute?
Do you notice any change in him?
Do you feel cold?
Do you object to smoking in cinemas?
Do you imagine she'll do it?

Example

TEACHER TO STUDENT A:	Ask him if the music sounds nice?
STUDENT A TO STUDENT B:	Does the music sound nice?
STUDENT B:	Yes, it does.
	(or) No, it doesn't.
*TEACHER TO STUDENT A:	What does he say?
STUDENT A:	He says the music sounds nice.
	He says the music doesn't sound nice.

*It should be possible to leave out 'What does he say?' after a few examples.

●*Drill*
Does the milk taste sour?
Does the fruit seem fresh?
Does the saucepan feel hot?
Does the coat cost much?
Does the soup smell good?
Does she sound French?
Does the price matter?
Does the bridge appear to be safe?
Does she seem friendly?
Does the car look new?
Does the coat suit me?
Does the colour match?
Does that book belong to you?

Example

TEACHER TO STUDENT A:	Ask him who he loves best.
STUDENT A TO STUDENT B:	Who do you love best?
STUDENT B:	I love (my mother) best.
*TEACHER TO STUDENT A:	What does he say?
STUDENT A:	He says he loves his mother best.

*It should be possible to leave out 'What does he say?' after a few examples.

Note The interrogative *Whom*? is found only in very formal writing and students should be strongly discouraged from using it in the spoken language.

● *Drill*

Which fruit do you like best?
What does *fast* mean?
Who does this book belong to?
Who does she remind you of?
How many books does the library contain?
How many pairs of shoes does she possess?
Which do you prefer, apples or pears?
What punishment does he deserve?
Where does he come from?
Who does he depend on?
Where do you believe he lives?
How many cigarettes does the box hold?
What nationality do you think he is?
How much does it cost?
Who does he look like?
How many houses does he own?
What does curry taste like?
What does silk feel like?
What does water consist of?
How many does he want?
What vegetable do you hate?
How much do you owe him?
What does *e.g.* stand for?
How many lessons does the course include?
Which book do you need, the red one or the blue one?
What qualifications do they require?
How many English people do you know?
What kind of people do you distrust?
Which parent does he resemble?
What does he refuse to do?

THE SIMPLE PAST

Elementary

To present the SIMPLE PAST *by means of actions.*

Method The teacher does the actions in group A, commenting as instructed. He then repeats the actions, asking after each one: 'What did I do?' The students answer: 'You . . .' (describing the action as the teacher described it before). The teacher should be sure that each action is completely finished before he comments or asks the question, and that the pronunciation of the verb ending (/t/, /d/, /id/) is as clear as possible without exaggeration.

When group A has been completed, the same procedure should be repeated with the other groups.

● *Drill*

(A) /t/ Verbs

The teacher walks across the room, returns to his desk, and then says:
      'I walked across the room.'

He picks up his pen from the desk, holds it up, puts it back on the desk, and then says:
      'I picked up my pen.'

He coughs, and then says:
      'I coughed.'

He picks up a book, looks at it, puts it down, and then says:
      'I looked at my book.'

He taps on the desk, and then says:
      'I tapped on the desk.'

(B) /t/ Verbs

He goes to the door, knocks, returns to his place, and then says:
      'I knocked on the door.'

He walks over to the window, looks out, returns to his place, and then says:
      'I looked out of the window.'

He selects a student, asks him a question, and then says:
      'I asked him a question.'

He laughs, and then says:
> 'I laughed.'

He drops a piece of chalk, picks it up, puts it on the desk, and then says:
> 'I dropped a piece of chalk.'

(C) /d/ Verbs

He picks up a closed book, opens it, closes it, and then says:
> I opened a book.'

He sneezes, and then says:
> 'I sneezed.'

He smiles at one of the students, and then says:
> 'I smiled at Miss X.'

He pulls up his sock, and then says:
> 'I pulled up my sock.'

He asks to borrow a pen from one of the students, takes it, writes in a book, gives the pen back, and then says:
> 'I borrowed a pen.'

(D) /id/ Verbs

He points at a student, and then says:
> 'I pointed at Mr Y.'

He lifts the table, and then says:
> 'I lifted the table.'

He takes a piece of paper, folds it, unfolds it, and then says:
> 'I folded a piece of paper.'

He takes some money out of his pocket, counts it, puts it back, and then says:
> 'I counted my money.'

He takes books from some of the students, gives them back, and then says:
> 'I collected some books.'

UNIT **14**   *Elementary*

To practise the pronunciation of the SIMPLE PAST

ENDINGS -d *and* -ed (/t/, /d/, /id/).

Method   The students answer the teacher's questions. The answers must consist of complete sentences and include the affirmative form of the verb used in the question. In the first two drills the teacher should pay special attention to the pronunciation of the link between the verb and the following word.

/t/ Verbs

>   *Example*
>   TEACHER: What did he jump over?
>   STUDENT: He jumped over the wall.

>   ●*Drill*
>   Did they walk on the pavement or in the road?
>   Who did he look at?
>   Did he ask his brother or his sister?
>   Where did they dance?
>   Did they talk in the library or in the classroom?
>   Where did the train stop?
>   Did she pick a red one or a blue one?
>   Where did John drop his book?
>   How long did Mary cook it?
>   Did he work in the house or in the garden?
>   When did he smoke a cigarette?
>   Did she practise in the afternoon or in the evening?
>   What time did they finish?
>   Where did Susan dress?
>   What did he knock over?
>   How many times did he help her?
>   When did he wash his hands?
>   When did he reach America?
>   What did he laugh at?
>   How long did he learn English?

/d/ Verbs

Example
TEACHER: When did it rain?
STUDENT: It rained in the morning.

● *Drill*
What time did the shop close?
How many times did he explain it?
Did you use a pen or a pencil?
Did you study Algebra or Arithmetic?
What time did the doors open?
Where did the children play?
Did he borrow it from you or your friend?
What time did they arrive?
What year did he die?
Did they stay in a hotel or in a private house?
What time did it happen?
When did he travel?
Where did he bathe?
How far did he carry it?
When did he marry her?
What time did John telephone?

/id/ Verbs

Example
TEACHER: When did Peter collect the books?
STUDENT: He collected them after the lesson.

● *Drill*
What time did we start the lesson?
Who did he point at?
How long did you wait for her?
How many times did he repeat it?
What time did the teacher end the lesson?
When did they expect the letter?
How many did he want?
When did the teacher correct the exercises?
When did John need the money?
When did they visit Mary?
Where did he mend the radio?
When did he count the money?
What did she knit?
What did he hate most?
How did he treat her?
Did he sound angry or pleased?

UNIT 15 *Elementary*

To *practise the form of the* SIMPLE PAST *with* REGULAR *and* IRREGULAR VERBS.

Note Part I practises Regular Verbs and Part II practises Irregular Verbs.

Example

*Stage One

TEACHER TO STUDENT A:	How long did you watch television last night?
STUDENT A:	I watched television for . . . hours last night.

Stage Two

TEACHER TO STUDENT B:	Ask A how long he watched television last night?
STUDENT B TO STUDENT A:	How long did you watch television last night?
STUDENT A:	I watched television for . . . hours last night.
*TEACHER TO STUDENT B:	What does he say?
STUDENT B:	He says he watched television for . . . hours last night.

Stage Three

TEACHER TO STUDENT B:	Ask him if he watched television for (different number) hours last night.
STUDENT B TO STUDENT A:	Did you watch television for (different number) hours last night?
STUDENT A:	No, I didn't.
*TEACHER TO STUDENT B:	What does he say?
STUDENT B:	He says he didn't watch television for (different number) hours last night.

*After a few examples, it should be possible to begin the drill with Stage Two. It should also be possible for the teacher to leave out 'What does he say?' once the students have grasped the form of the drill.

Part I *Regular Verbs*

●*Drill*

How many hours did you work yesterday?
How many days did you attend school last week?
How many times did you telephone your friend last week?
How many times did you clean your teeth yesterday?
How many times did you wash your hands yesterday?
How long did you boil the egg?
How long did you cook the meat?
How much money did you receive?
How far did you walk?
How often did you visit your friend last week?

What did you use to write your homework?
What did you carry your books in?
What did you cook for dinner?
What did you drop on the floor?
What colour did you paint the house?
What subjects did you study last year?
What flowers did you pick in the garden?

What time did you arrive at school?
What time did you start lessons?
What time did you stop for (coffee)?
What time did you finish classes?

Where did you drop your book?
Where did you play football?
Where did you wait for your friend?
Where did you walk to?

When did you arrive in (England)?
When did you start at this school?
When did you receive a letter from (your parents)?
When did you telephone your friend?

With a class that has thoroughly grasped the procedure of the drill, it should be possible to practise the last three sections with call-words only.

Example

TEACHER TO STUDENT A:	switch on the radio
STUDENT A TO STUDENT B:	What time did you switch on the radio?
STUDENT B:	I switched on the radio at 7.30.
STUDENT A:	He says he switched on the radio at 7.30.
TEACHER TO STUDENT A:	8.30
STUDENT A TO STUDENT B:	Did you switch on the radio at 8.30?
STUDENT B:	No, I didn't.
STUDENT A:	He says he didn't switch on the radio at 8.30.

Part II *Irregular Verbs*

●*Drill*

How many times did you go to the cinema last month?
How did you come to school?
How many meals did you eat yesterday?
How much did you pay for that (book)?
How long did you sit in the classroom yesterday?
How much time did you spend on your homework yesterday?
How many cups of coffee did you drink yesterday?
How did you feel yesterday?

What did you drink after lunch yesterday?
What did you have for breakfast this morning?
What did you get for your birthday?
What did you find in your pocket?

What bus did you catch to school this morning?
What cinema did you go to at the weekend?
What colour did you choose?
What language did you speak to him in?

What time did you get up this morning?
What time did you leave for school yesterday?
What time did you begin lessons yesterday?
What time did you have lunch yesterday?

Where did you have breakfast this morning?
Where did you go for your holidays last year?
Where did you buy that book?
Where did you catch the bus?

When did you do your homework yesterday?
When did you light the fire?
When did you meet your boy-(girl-)friend?
When did you buy your car?

As in Part I, it should be possible to practise the last three sections with call-words only.

UNIT **16**   *Elementary, Intermediate and Advanced*

To practise the SIMPLE PAST *of* IRREGULAR VERBS.

Note The questions in Sections A to E practise the past forms of most of the Irregular Verbs that students are likely to need. The teacher should make sure that the students have thoroughly mastered the forms in one section before going on to the next. Section F practises verbs with unchanging past forms, which may be practised at the same time as those in other sections, at the discretion of the teacher. He may also decide to omit the final verbs in Sections E and F as being too infrequent to justify inclusion.

Section A   ●*Drill*
What time did this lesson begin?
When did you come to (England)?
When did she do the washing-up?
Did he get a good mark or a bad mark for his exercise?
Where did you find that £5 note?
How much money did you give him?
Did he go to the cinema or to the theatre?

When did you hear that story?
Where did she keep her books?
How many English words did she know?
How many mistakes did he make?
How many books did she read last month?
Did you say 'yes' or 'no'?
Where did he see her?
Did you sit at the front or at the back of the cinema?
How long did they stand at the bus-stop?
Where did she take her brother?
Did she tell the story well or badly?
Did you think of it yesterday or today?
How many lines did she write?

Section B

How many books did he bring?
Where did he buy that book?
Did he drink beer or whisky in the pub?
What did you eat for dinner last night?
When did you fall down the stairs?
Did you feel happy or sad last night?
How many words did you forget?
Did he hold the pen in his right hand or in his left hand?
Where did you learn to drive?
What time did you leave home this morning?
What time did she light the fire?
Did his answer mean 'yes' or 'no'?
What time did you meet him last night?
How much did he pay for his car?
How many times did he ring the bell?
Where did he run to?
When did he sell his old car?
How much money did he send her?
Did he speak quickly or slowly?
Did he teach you French or German?
Did he understand all the lesson or only half of it?

Section C

How many teeth did he break?
How many houses did they build last year?
Did he catch a big fish or a little one?
Did she choose coffee or tea?
What did he draw a picture of?
How far did you drive in his car?
Where did the two men fight?
Did he grow flowers or vegetables in his garden?
How long did you lie in bed this morning?

Where did you lose your ring?
How many times did you ride in their car?
How many songs did she sing?
Did you sleep well or badly?
How many hours did the sun shine yesterday?
Did the meat smell good or bad?
How much money did you spend in the restaurant?
Who did the motorist swear at?
How long did she swim in the sea?
What time did you wake up this morning?
What did she wear last night?
How much money did he win?
When did he wind up his watch?

Section D

When did Mr . . . become Prime Minister?
How many iron bars did the strong man bend?
How many times did the guard blow his whistle?
What did you burn your fingers on?
What did you dream about last night?
Did he fly to Rome or to New York?
How many times did you forgive him?
Where did she hang the picture?
Where did he hide the money?
How many eggs did the chicken lay?
Where did the road lead to?
How long did he lean against the wall?
How much money did he lend you?
What time did the sun rise this morning?
How many birds did he shoot?
Did she spell the word correctly or wrongly?
How much money did they steal?
How many stamps did he stick on the letter?
How many pages did he tear out of his book?
Did he throw the ball to his brother or to his sister?

Section E

How many times did the dog bite him?
What time did you creep up the stairs last night?
How many letters did the secretary deal with yesterday?
How many trees did the men dig up?
When did she feed the chickens?
Where did his father forbid him to go?
When did the lake freeze?
Did the miller grind the wheat or the barley?
Where did she kneel?
How many inches did the curtains shrink?
How many times did you shake the medicine?
When did the ship sink?
Did he slide on his feet or on his behind?
Did you spill coffee or tea on your suit?

> How many times did the roulette wheel spin round?
> Where did the old man spit?
> Which child did she spoil?
> Where did the lion spring from?
> How many people did the wasps sting?
> How many matches did he strike?
> How many times did she sweep the floor?
> How many times did he swing the rope round his head?
> What did he tread on?
> Where did she weep?

The following may also be practised:

> How long did your nose bleed?
> Did he breed horses or dogs?
> Did they bind his wrists with string or rope?
> What did the drowning man cling to?
> Did the man flee to Switzerland or to Portugal?
> Did she fling his letter into the fire or into the waste-paper basket?
> Who did he forsake?
> How many hurdles did the runner leap over?
> Where did he seek shelter?
> Where did he sling his hammock?
> What did he strive to do?
> What did the kitchen stink of?
> Did he stride into the office or into the canteen?

Section F

> Who did you beat at tennis yesterday?
> How much did you bet on the horse?
> When did your water-pipes burst?
> How much did that book cost?
> Did he cut the paper with scissors or a knife?
> Where did he hit you?
> Did he hurt his right arm or his left?
> When did the teacher let you go home?
> Where did she put her cigarette?
> What time did you set your alarm-clock for?
> What time did he shut the restaurant?
> What did you spread on your piece of toast?
> Did he upset his mother or his father by his rudeness?

The following may also be practised:

> How much did he bid for the antique table?
> How many times did the fisherman cast his line into the water?
> What did he thrust into your hand?
> What did he slit the letter open with?
> How many pieces did the wood split into?

| UNIT **17** | *Intermediate* |

To practise the pattern: It's . . . (*length of time*) since

+ SIMPLE PAST.

Example
TEACHER: The last time he smoked a cigarette was two years ago.
STUDENT: It's two years since he smoked a cigarette.

●*Drill*
The last time I saw them was a fortnight ago.
The last time she went to the hairdresser was three weeks ago.
The last time she drove her car was a year ago.
The last time he had a glass of champagne was months ago.
The last time we travelled on a bus was weeks ago.
The last time I listened to the radio was four days ago.
The last time he spoke German was a long time ago.
The last time we met her was a month ago.
The last time I gave a party was a year ago.
The last time I read a newspaper was three days ago.
The last time she did her homework was three weeks ago.
The last time he came to class was a week ago.
The last time I wrote any exercises was ten days ago.
The last time we travelled by air was five years ago.
The last time I played cards was over a year ago.
The last time she helped me was three weeks ago.
The last time we had lunch with them was a fortnight ago.
The last time he was on time was ages ago.
The last time he took her out was three weeks ago.
The last time I received a letter was over a month ago.

UNIT 18   *Intermediate*

To practise the SIMPLE PAST *with* when *to make a statement about two* CONSECUTIVE PAST ACTIONS.

Method   The teacher asks the following questions and the students answer, using the cues provided, as in the first example.

When the drill has been done in this way, the two parts of the sentences may be reversed, as in the second example.

Note   This Unit should be used in conjunction with Unit 26.

Example 1
TEACHER: When did he have his dinner?   get home
STUDENT: He had his dinner when he got home.

Example 2
TEACHER: What happened when he got home?
STUDENT: When he got home, he had his dinner.

●*Drill*

When did you see him?	come in
When did he break his leg?	fall downstairs
When did he cut himself?	pick up the knife
When did he notice it?	look up
When did the car stop?	run out of petrol
When did she drop the plate?	trip over
When did he start coughing?	light a cigarette
When did the doctor come?	get the message
When did you find it?	open the drawer
When did he bump his head?	stand up
When did he hurt his back?	slip on the ice
When did she burn herself?	touch the heater
When did he smile?	see her
When did the car run off the road?	tyre/burst
When did she go to bed?	mother/tell her
When did you stop writing?	pencil/break

When did they come in?   rain/start
When did she turn off the television?   news/begin
When did she injure her arm?   car/crash
When did you take off your coat?   sun/come out
When did the train start?   guard/blow his whistle
When did he go to the door?   bell/ring
When did you stop work?   clock/strike seven
When did she switch off the radio?   programme/finish
When did the traffic move off?   lights/change

Both forms of this drill may be practised with short answers.

Examples
TEACHER: When did he have his dinner?
STUDENT: When he got home.
TEACHER: What happened when he got home?
STUDENT: He had his dinner.

UNIT **19**   *Elementary*

To practise the SIMPLE PAST *used for a* HABIT.

Method The teacher explains to the students that he is going to ask
them some questions about their habits at certain times in the past. He
introduces each section separately before asking the questions that follow,
telling the students to think back to the given times.

●*Drill*
Section A   Questions about last term.
Did you work well or badly at school last term?
Did you behave well or badly at school last term?
Did you walk to school or did you go by bus last term?
What languages did you study last term?
How many English lessons did you have every week last term?
What other subjects did you learn last term?
How many hours homework did you do each day last term?
Did you get good marks or bad marks for your work last term?
What days did you play games last term?
What games did you play?

Section B   Questions about last week.
Did you have lunch at home or in a restaurant last Saturday?
Did you wear a cardigan or a sweater most days last week?
Did you come to school by bus last week, or did you walk?
Did you arrive at school early or late last Friday?
How long did you spend on your homework each evening last week?

Section C　Questions about holidays.

Did you get up early or late during your holiday?
Did you go to bed early or late during your holiday?
Did you usually have an early or a late breakfast during your holiday?
What time did you come in for lunch during your holiday?
How often did you wash your hair during your holiday?
How many times did you go dancing in the evening during your holiday?
Did you sleep well or badly during your holiday?
Did you usually have a swim before or after breakfast during your holiday?
How long did you lie on the beach every day during your holiday?
What time did you meet your friends every day during your holiday?

The following section may also be used if the students are studying English outside their own country.

Section D　Questions about the student's past life in his country.

What did you do when you were a child?
What did you do when you were at school?
What did you do during the holidays when you were at school?
What day did your father give you your pocket money?
How many parties did you go to every year?
How often did you go to the cinema in your country?
What did you do during the evenings when you were at home?
What evenings did you go out?
How many meals did you have every day?
What did you do at the weekends when you were at home?
What did you drink with your meals?
How much money did you spend every week?
How often did you eat out in your country?
How often did you travel by train in your country?
What days did you have free in your country?

THE PAST CONTINUOUS

To contrast the PRESENT CONTINUOUS *with the* PAST

CONTINUOUS.

Method The teacher says a sentence using *At the moment* with the
Present Continuous. The students repeat this and then change the time
and tense, using *At this time yesterday* with the Past Continuous.

Example

TEACHER: At the moment he's drinking a glass of whisky.
STUDENT: At the moment he's drinking a glass of whisky.
         At *this time yesterday* he was drinking a glass of whisky.

●*Drill*

At the moment she's listening to the teacher.
Now we're sitting in the classroom.
At the moment she's writing a composition.
Now he's speaking English.
At the moment I'm doing an exercise.
Now Mary's doing the washing-up.
At the moment Mother's making the beds.
Now she's wearing her new dress.
At the moment Jane's doing the shopping.
Now the teacher's teaching us.
At the moment he's reading the newspaper.
Now we're working in class.
At the moment he's taking the dog out for a walk.
Now she's preparing the lunch.
At the moment Mr Smith's playing golf.
Now they're paying attention to the lesson.
At the moment Father's having a rest.
Now we're learning English.
At the moment the secretary's typing letters.
Now he's thinking about his holiday.

UNIT **21**   *Elementary*

To practise the form of the PAST CONTINUOUS *(affirmative and negative).*

Note   There is a change of form in Part II of the drill.

Part I

●*Drill*

TEACHER TO STUDENT A:	Ask me what I was doing at two o'clock.
STUDENT A TO TEACHER:	What were you doing at two o'clock.
TEACHER:	I was coming to school.
	What was I doing at two o'clock?
STUDENT A:	You were coming to school.
TEACHER TO STUDENT A:	Ask me if I was eating my lunch at two o'clock.
STUDENT A TO TEACHER:	Were you eating your lunch at two o'clock?'
TEACHER:	No, I wasn't.
	Was I eating my lunch at two o'clock?
STUDENT A:	No, you weren't.
TEACHER TO STUDENT B:	What does he say?
STUDENT B:	He says you weren't eating your lunch at two o'clock.
TEACHER TO STUDENT B:	Ask me what I was doing at four o'clock yesterday.
STUDENT B TO TEACHER:	What were you doing at four o'clock yesterday?
TEACHER:	I was teaching my class.
	What was I doing at four o'clock yesterday?
STUDENT B:	You were teaching your class.
TEACHER TO STUDENT B:	Ask me if I was having a rest at four o'clock yesterday.
STUDENT B TO TEACHER:	Were you having a rest at four o'clock yesterday?
TEACHER:	No, I wasn't.
	Was I having a rest at four o'clock yesterday?
STUDENT B:	No, you weren't.
TEACHER TO STUDENT C:	What does he say?
STUDENT C:	He says you weren't having a rest at four o'clock yesterday.
TEACHER TO STUDENT C:	Ask me what I was doing at half past eight this morning.
STUDENT C:	What were you doing at half past eight this morning?
TEACHER:	I was finishing my breakfast.
	What was I doing at half past eight this morning?
STUDENT C:	You were finishing your breakfast.

TEACHER TO STUDENT C:	Ask me if I was getting into bed at half past eight.
STUDENT C:	Were you getting into bed at half past eight?
TEACHER:	No, I wasn't.
	Was I getting into bed at half past eight?
STUDENT C TO TEACHER:	No, you weren't.
TEACHER TO STUDENT D:	What does he say?
STUDENT D:	He says you weren't getting into bed at half past eight this morning.
TEACHER TO STUDENT D:	Ask me what I was doing at half past ten yesterday morning.
STUDENT D:	What were you doing at half past ten yesterday morning?
TEACHER:	I was giving a lesson. etc.
TEACHER TO STUDENT D:	Ask me if I was sitting in a restaurant at half past ten yesterday morning.
STUDENT D:	Were you sitting in a restaurant at half past ten yesterday morning? etc.
TEACHER TO STUDENT E:	Ask me what I was doing at six o'clock yesterday evening.
STUDENT E:	What were you doing at six o'clock yesterday evening?
TEACHER:	I was having my tea. etc.
TEACHER TO STUDENT E:	Ask me if I was having my lunch at six o'clock yesterday evening.
STUDENT E:	Were you having your lunch at six o'clock yesterday evening? etc.
TEACHER TO STUDENT F:	Ask me what I was doing in the coffee bar.
STUDENT F:	What were you doing in the coffee bar?
TEACHER:	I was drinking a cup of coffee. etc.
TEACHER TO STUDENT F:	Ask me if I was drinking whisky.
STUDENT F:	Were you drinking whisky? etc.
TEACHER TO STUDENT G:	Ask me what I was doing at the railway station.
STUDENT G:	What were you doing at the railway station?
TEACHER:	I was buying a ticket. etc.
TEACHER TO STUDENT G:	Ask me if I was waiting for a friend.
STUDENT G:	Were you waiting for a friend? etc.
TEACHER TO STUDENT H:	Ask me what I was doing in the restaurant.
STUDENT H:	What were you doing in the restaurant?
TEACHER:	I was having a meal. etc.
TEACHER TO STUDENT H:	Ask me if I was writing letters.
STUDENT H:	Were you writing letters? etc.
TEACHER TO STUDENT I:	Ask me what I was doing in the cinema.
STUDENT I:	What were you doing in the cinema?
TEACHER:	I was seeing a film. etc.

TEACHER TO STUDENT I:	Ask me if I was seeing the film for the second time.
STUDENT I:	Were you seeing the film for the second time? etc.
TEACHER TO STUDENT J:	Ask me what I was doing at the dance hall.
STUDENT J:	What were you doing at the dance hall?
TEACHER:	I was dancing. etc.
TEACHER TO STUDENT J:	Ask me if I was playing in the band.
STUDENT J:	Were you playing in the band? etc.

Part II

● *Drill*

TEACHER TO STUDENT A:	Ask him what he was doing at one o'clock.
STUDENT A TO STUDENT B:	What were you doing at one o'clock?
STUDENT B:	(I was eating my lunch.)
TEACHER TO STUDENT A:	What does he say?
STUDENT A:	He says he was eating his lunch.
TEACHER TO STUDENT A:	Ask him if he was sleeping at one o'clock.
STUDENT A TO STUDENT B:	Were you sleeping at one o'clock.
STUDENT B:	No, I wasn't.
TEACHER TO STUDENT A:	What does he say?
STUDENT A:	He says he wasn't sleeping at one o'clock.
TEACHER TO STUDENT B:	Ask him what he was doing at five o'clock this morning.
STUDENT B TO STUDENT C:	What were you doing at five o'clock this morning?
STUDENT C:	(I was sleeping.)
TEACHER TO STUDENT B:	What does he say?
STUDENT B:	He says he was sleeping.
TEACHER TO STUDENT B:	Ask him if he was cleaning his shoes at five o'clock.
STUDENT B TO STUDENT C:	Were you cleaning your shoes at five o'clock?
STUDENT C:	No, I wasn't.
TEACHER TO STUDENT B:	What does he say?
STUDENT B:	He says he wasn't cleaning his shoes at five o'clock this morning.
TEACHER TO STUDENT C:	Ask him what he was doing at eight o'clock this morning.
STUDENT C TO STUDENT D:	What were you doing at eight o'clock this morning?
STUDENT D:	I was . . . ing. etc.
TEACHER TO STUDENT C:	Ask him if he was going to bed at eight o'clock this morning.
STUDENT C TO STUDENT D:	Were you going to bed at eight o'clock this morning? etc.

TEACHER TO STUDENT D:	Ask him what he was doing at eleven o'clock last night.
STUDENT D TO STUDENT E:	What were you doing at eleven o'clock last night?
STUDENT E:	I was . . . ing. etc.
TEACHER TO STUDENT D:	Ask him if he was getting up.
STUDENT D TO STUDENT E:	Were you getting up at eleven o'clock last night? etc
TEACHER TO STUDENT E:	Ask him what he was doing at eight o'clock yesterday morning.
STUDENT E TO STUDENT F:	What were you doing at eight o'clock yesterday morning?
STUDENT F:	I was . . . ing. etc.
TEACHER TO STUDENT E:	Ask him if he was sitting in the classroom.
STUDENT E TO STUDENT F:	Were you sitting in the classroom at eight o'clock yesterday morning? etc.
TEACHER TO STUDENT F:	Ask him what he was doing in the art gallery.
STUDENT F TO STUDENT G:	What were you doing in the art gallery?
STUDENT G:	I was . . . ing. etc.
TEACHER TO STUDENT F:	Ask him if he was reading.
STUDENT F TO STUDENT G:	Were you reading? etc.
TEACHER TO STUDENT G:	Ask him what he was doing in the Indian Restaurant.
STUDENT G TO STUDENT H:	What were you doing in the Indian Restaurant?
STUDENT H:	I was . . . ing. etc.
TEACHER TO STUDENT G:	Ask him if he was eating a Chinese meal.
STUDENT G TO STUDENT H:	Were you eating a Chinese meal? etc.
TEACHER TO STUDENT H:	Ask him what he was doing in the library.
STUDENT H TO STUDENT I:	What were you doing in the library?
STUDENT I:	I was . . . ing. etc.
TEACHER TO STUDENT H:	Ask him if he was playing the piano.
STUDENT H TO STUDENT I:	Were you playing the piano? etc.
TEACHER TO STUDENT I:	Ask him what he was doing at the airport.
STUDENT I TO STUDENT J:	What were you doing at the airport?
STUDENT J:	I was . . . ing. etc.
TEACHER TO STUDENT I:	Ask him if he was making an enquiry.
STUDENT I TO STUDENT J:	Were you making an enquiry? etc.
TEACHER TO STUDENT J:	Ask him what he was doing at the bus stop.
STUDENT J TO STUDENT K:	What were you doing at the bus stop?
STUDENT K:	I was . . . ing. etc.
TEACHER TO STUDENT J:	Ask him if he was waiting for a taxi.
STUDENT J TO STUDENT K:	Were you waiting for a taxi? etc.

Part II of the drill on the previous page may also be practised with call-words.

Example

TEACHER TO STUDENT A:	Seven o'clock this morning.
STUDENT A TO STUDENT B:	What were you doing at seven o'clock this morning?
STUDENT B:	I was dressing.
STUDENT A:	He says he was dressing.
TEACHER TO STUDENT A:	Having breakfast.
STUDENT A TO STUDENT B:	Were you having breakfast?
STUDENT B:	No, I wasn't.
STUDENT A:	He says he wasn't having breakfast.

UNIT **22**   *Elementary and Intermediate*

To practise the PAST CONTINUOUS *after* because.

Method   The teacher gives the stimulus, which the students repeat and complete, using the cues provided with the verb in the Past Continuous, as in the example.

Example

TEACHER: She didn't come to school because she . . .   feel ill
STUDENT: She didn't come to school because she was feeling ill.

●*Drill*

She didn't hear the bell because she . . .	sleep
He had an accident because he . . .	drive too fast
He wouldn't go out because he . . .	study for an exam
She didn't hear the phone because she . . .	listen to the radio
He couldn't run because he . . .	carry a heavy case
They never went out because they . . .	save for a new car
She didn't go to the party because she . . .	feel tired
I got wet because it . . .	rain
The teacher was angry because the students . . .	talk
We didn't talk because he . . .	play a record
I had to wait because she . . .	do her homework
He told us to be quiet because he . . .	watch the television
I couldn't speak to him on the phone because he . . .	have a bath
He looked very smart because he . . .	wear a new suit
She didn't hear what I said because she . . .	read
We had to go out because Susan . . .	practise her violin
I couldn't hear what he was saying because I . . .	sit at the back
She didn't want to leave the party because she . .	enjoy herself

The following examples may be practised with more advanced students.

She couldn't walk very far because she . . .	wear high-heeled shoes
She looked untidy because the wind . . .	blow her hair about
He couldn't leave the house because he . . .	wait for a telephone call
The children were afraid because it . . .	get dark
There was a strong smell because the cook . . .	fry onions
He choked because he . . .	eat too quickly
The police stopped him because he . . .	exceed the speed limit
He scorched his trousers because he . . .	stand too near the fire
His room was untidy because he . . .	sort out his papers
The roads were crowded because a lot of people . . .	go on holiday
He stayed awake half the night because he . . .	sleep in a strange bed
I stopped the car because someone . . .	lie in the road
The dog started to bark because someone . . .	try to get in the house
I couldn't see the name of the station because the train . . .	travel too fast
He took the radio to pieces because it . . .	make a funny noise

---

UNIT **23**   *Elementary and Intermediate*

To introduce by means of actions the pattern: while + *the*
PAST CONTINUOUS (*for an Unfinished Action*) *contrasted*
with the SIMPLE PAST (*for a Finished Action*).

Method   The teacher does the actions in group A, commenting on each
one after he has completed it. He then repeats the actions for the students
to make the comments: 'While you were . . ., you . . .' When group A has
been completed, the same procedure should be repeated with groups B
and C.

● *Drill*

(A)   While I was crossing the room, I dropped my pen.
     While I was writing, my chalk broke.
     While I was reading, I blew my nose.
     While I was looking for my keys, I found my pencil.
     While I was looking through the magazine, I tore a page.

(B)   While I was reading, I looked at my watch.
While I was crossing the room, I tripped over the mat.
While I was reading, I sneezed.
While I was looking at my book, I scratched my head.
While I was wiping the board, I dropped the duster.

(C)   While he was reading, I spoke to him.
While you were looking at your books, I switched on the light.
While you were writing, I closed/opened the window.
While he was looking the other way, I took his pen.
While she was copying the sentence, I rubbed it off the board.

UNIT **24**   *Elementary and Intermediate*

To practise the pattern: while/when + *the* PAST

CONTINUOUS (*for an Unfinished Action*) *contrasted with*

the SIMPLE PAST (*for a Finished Action*).

Example
TEACHER: What did he tear when he was climbing the tree?
STUDENT: When he was climbing the tree, he tore his trousers.

● *Drill*
What did she break while she was washing up?
What did he see when he was looking out of the window?
What did he find when he was looking for his gloves?
What did he read while he was waiting to see the dentist?
What did she drop when she was running downstairs?
What did he lose while he was walking in the park?
Who did she meet when she was shopping?
Who did he see when he was standing outside the cinema?
Who did he write to when he was staying in France?

Example
TEACHER: What happened while you were decorating the sitting room?
STUDENT: While I was decorating the sitting room, I knocked over the
           paint.

● *Drill*
What happened while you were watching television?
What happened while you were sitting in the park?
What happened while you were spending your holidays in France?
What happened while you were having a bath?

What happened when you were flying over the Alps?
What happened when he was shaving?
What happened when you were driving fast round a bend?
What happened while your aunt was walking in the park?
What happened when the gardener was digging in the garden?
What happened while you were standing outside the cinema?
What happened while she was cooking the lunch?
What happened when he was drinking his coffee?
What happened while you were having tea?
What happened while he was waiting for his girl-friend?
What happened when she was running downstairs?

Example
TEACHER: When did you finish the box of chocolates?
STUDENT: I finished the box of chocolates while/when I was watching television.

● *Drill*
When did he cut himself?
When did she have the accident?
When did he break his leg?
When did the car break down?
When did she drop the plate?
When did you lose your way?
When did they visit Westminster Abbey?
When did he start coughing?
When did she fall asleep?
When did the postman come?
When did they arrive?
When did he meet her?
When did you find it?
When did he take the exam?
When did you see him?

The last section of the above drill may then be repeated to get short answers from the students.

Example
TEACHER: When did you finish the box of chocolates?
STUDENT: While/When I was watching television.

UNIT 25 *Elementary and Intermediate*

To practise the pattern: when + *the* SIMPLE PAST (*for a Finished Action*) *contrasted with the* PAST CONTINUOUS (*for an Unfinished Action*).

Example

TEACHER: What was he thinking about when she called him?
STUDENT: When she called him, he was thinking about his holiday.

● *Drill*

What car was he driving when he had the accident?
What was she knitting when you went to see her?
What record was he playing when the visitors arrived?
What was Rosemary cooking when the children got back from school?
What book was he reading when the telephone rang?
What was the carpenter making when you went into the workshop?
What was the secretary typing when the manager rushed into the office?
What was she ironing when her husband came home?
What was he talking about when she interrupted him?

Example

TEACHER: What were they doing when the letter arrived?
STUDENT: When the letter arrived, they were having breakfast.

● *Drill*

What were you doing when the telephone rang?
What was she doing when her friend arrived?
What was he doing when you knocked at the door?
What were they doing when it began to rain?
What was she doing when the train came in?
What were you doing when the teacher came into the room?
What was the gardener doing when you went into the garden?
What was the driver doing when the car crashed?
What was the teacher doing when you arrived at school?
What was the bus-conductor doing when you got on his bus?
What was your friend doing when you arrived at his house?

The above drill may then be repeated to get shorter answers from the students.

Example

TEACHER: What were they doing when the letter arrived?
STUDENT: They were having breakfast.

UNIT **26**	*Intermediate*

To contrast (a) *a statement with one verb in the* SIMPLE

PAST *and one in the* PAST CONTINUOUS *with* (b) *a*

statement with two verbs in the SIMPLE PAST.

Note   This unit should be used in conjunction with Unit 18.

Example

TEACHER: What were you doing when you heard the burglar?
STUDENT: When I heard the burglar, I was reading in bed.
TEACHER: What did you do when you heard the burglar?
STUDENT: When I heard the burglar, I telephoned the police.

●*Drill*

What were you doing when it began to rain?
What did you do when it began to rain?

What were they doing when the teacher came into the room?
What did they do when the teacher came into the room?

What were you doing when he offered you a cigarette?
What did you do when he offered you a cigarette?

What was she doing when the train arrived?
What did she do when the train arrived?

What was he doing when the telephone rang?
What did he do when the telephone rang?

What were you doing when you met your friend?
What did you do when you met your friend?

What were they doing when the letters arrived?
What did they do when the letters arrived?

What were you doing when he opened the window?
What did you do when he opened the window?

What was she doing when she cut her finger?
What did she do when she cut her finger?

What were they doing when the lights went out?
What did they do when the lights went out?

What were you doing when you lost your way?
What did you do when you lost your way?

What was he doing when he heard the good news?
What did he do when he heard the good news?

What were you doing when she turned on the television?
What did you do when she turned on the television?

What were you doing when the film started?
What did you do when the film started?

What was he doing when he sneezed?
What did he do when he sneezed?

What were they doing when he knocked at the door?
What did they do when he knocked at the door?

What were you doing when your pen ran out?
What did you do when your pen ran out?

What was she doing when she smashed the plate?
What did she do when she smashed the plate?

When the contrast between the two statements has been thoroughly practised, the above drill may then be repeated to get shorter answers from the students.

Example
TEACHER: What were you doing when you heard the burglar?
STUDENT: I was reading in bed.
TEACHER: What did you do when you heard the burglar?
STUDENT: I telephoned the police.

UNIT **27**   *Intermediate*

To introduce, by means of actions, the SIMPLE PAST

followed by just as *and the* PAST CONTINUOUS.

Method   The teacher organises the following situations, commenting on each one after completing it. The demonstrations are then repeated, and the students are required to make the comments.

● *Drill*
I sneezed just as I was starting the drill.
I took his pen away just as he was beginning to write.
I closed his book just as he was starting to read.
I called him back just as he was going out of the room.
My chalk broke just as I was beginning to write.
I stopped him just as he was closing the door.
I snatched the book just as he was passing it to her.
I coughed just as I was starting to speak.
I got a pain in my leg just as I was standing up.
I turned my back just as he was going to ask a question.

UNIT **28** *Intermediate*

To practise the SIMPLE PAST *followed by* just as *and the*

PAST CONTINUOUS.

Method The teacher asks the following questions, which the students answer with *just as* and the Past Continuous, using the cues provided, as in the example. (These cues are also used for the next drill.)

Example
TEACHER: When did the phone ring? get into the bath
STUDENT: The phone rang just as I was getting into the bath.

● *Drill*

When did it begin to rain?	leave the house
When did your pen run out?	begin to write
When did the baker call?	go out
When did the telegram arrive?	sit down to lunch
When did the alarm ring?	drop off to sleep
When did the teacher come in?	start to draw on the board
When did your friends arrive?	get out of the bath
When did the telephone ring?	put on my coat
When did the lights fuse?	finish dinner
When did you run out of petrol?	leave the town
When did they come round to see you?	begin supper
When did he ask her to dance?	leave
When did David come home?	lock up
When did the phone go?	get undressed
When did the rain start?	get off the train
When did he call you back?	open the gate
When did the train leave?	rush into the station
When did he fall ill?	go on holiday
When did the baby start to cry?	put out the lights
When did your brother come in?	pour out the tea

The above drill may then be repeated to get shorter answers from the students.

Example
TEACHER: When did the phone ring?
STUDENT: Just as I was getting into the bath.

The teacher may then get the students to ask questions using the cues, beginning 'What happened . . .?'

Example
STUDENT A: What happened just as you were getting into the bath?
STUDENT B: The phone rang.

UNIT **29**   *Intermediate*

To practise when *and the* SIMPLE PAST *with the* PAST CONTINUOUS *and* just.

Method   The teacher asks the following questions, which the students answer with the Past Continuous and *just*, using the cues provided, as in the example. (These cues are also used for the preceding drill.)

Example

TEACHER :   What were you doing when the phone rang?   get into the bath
STUDENT :   When the phone rang, I was just getting into the bath.

● *Drill*

What were you doing when it began to rain?	leave the house
What were you doing when your pen ran out?	begin to write
What were you doing when the baker called?	go out
What were you doing when the telegram arrived?	sit down to lunch
What were you doing when the alarm rang?	drop off to sleep
What were you doing when the teacher came in?	start to draw on the board
What were you doing when your friends arrived?	get out of the bath
What were you doing when the telephone rang?	put on my coat
What were you doing when the lights fused?	finish dinner
What were you doing when you ran out of petrol?	leave the town
What were you doing when they came round to see you?	begin supper
What was she doing when he asked her to dance?	leave
What were you doing when David came home?	lock up
What were you doing when the phone went?	get undressed
What were you doing when he called you back?	open the gate
What were you doing when the train left?	rush into the station
What was he doing when he fell ill?	go on holiday

The above drill may then be repeated to get shorter answers from the students.

Example

TEACHER :   What were you doing when the phone rang?
STUDENT :   I was just getting into the bath.

In order to get the pattern reversed, the teacher may present the Simple Past as the stimulus.

Example

TEACHER :   . . . the phone rang.
STUDENT :   I was just getting into the bath when the phone rang.

UNIT **30**   *Intermediate*

To introduce, by means of actions, while *with two*

SIMULTANEOUS *and* CONTRASTED ACTIONS *in the* PAST

CONTINUOUS.

Method   The teacher does or organises the actions in group A, commenting on each one after it is completed. The actions are then repeated for the students to make the comments. The same procedure is then repeated for the other groups.

● *Drill*

(A)   While I was standing on my right leg, he was standing on his left leg.
      While he was looking out of the window, I was looking at my book.
      While I was holding up my left hand, he was holding up his right hand.
      While I was writing with a pen, he was writing with a pencil.
      While he was pointing at the door, she was pointing at the window.

(B)   While I was drawing a house, he was drawing a ship.
      While he was shaking hands with Mr X, I was shaking hands with Mr Y.
      While he was holding up a book, she was holding up a pen.
      While I was reading a newspaper, he was reading a magazine.
      While he was walking to the door, she was walking to the window.

(C)   While I was sitting down, he was standing up.
      While he was reading, I was listening to him.
      While I was crying, he was laughing.
      While you were reading from your book, I was writing on the blackboard.
      While I was writing on the blackboard, you were watching me.

(D)   While I was singing, you were whistling.
      While I was putting my jacket on, he was taking his jacket off.
      While he was reading a book, she was writing a letter.
      While he was cleaning the window, I was polishing the desk.
      While he was looking through his dictionary, she was counting her money.

UNIT 31   *Intermediate*

To practise while all the time *with two* SIMULTANEOUS

and CONTRASTED ACTIONS *in the* PAST CONTINUOUS.

Example

TEACHER: What were you doing while your friend was doing his homework?

STUDENT: While my friend was doing his homework, I was watching television.

●*Drill*

What were you doing while I was resting?

What were you doing while John was cleaning his bicycle?

What were you doing while she was writing letters?

What was she doing while he was taking his exam?

What was he doing while she was preparing the lunch?

What were you doing while the boys were doing their homework?

What were you doing while he was digging in the garden?

What was she doing while they were looking at the photographs?

What was Mrs Brown doing while Mr Brown was playing the violin?

What were you doing while your father was typing his letters?

What were they doing while I was playing the gramophone?

What were you doing while she was making the beds?

What were you doing while he was cleaning the car?

What was she doing while he was drinking whisky?

What was the child doing while his mother was getting the lunch?

Example

TEACHER: What were you doing all the time she was getting the coffee?

STUDENT: All the time she was getting the coffee, I was playing with the baby.

●*Drill*

What were you doing all the time he was talking on the phone?

What was he doing all the time she was having a bath?

What were they doing all the time you were cooking the lunch?

What was he doing all the time she was putting the children to bed?

What were you doing all the time he was saying good-night to his girlfriend?

What were they doing all the time the record was playing?

What was he doing all the time she was doing her hair?

What was the dog doing all the time the man was working?

What were you doing all the time he was writing his letters?

What was she doing all the time you were getting the tea?

What was he doing all the time she was having her hair done?

What was she doing all the time they were talking to their friends?

What were the students doing all the time the teacher was writing on the blackboard?

What was the husband doing all the time his wife was walking round the shops?

What was he doing all the time she was getting ready?

The above drills may then be repeated to get shorter answers.

Example
TEACHER: What were you doing while your friend was doing his homework?
STUDENT: I was watching television.

UNIT **32** *Elementary*

To practise the PAST CONTINUOUS *for a* LONG-LASTING

PAST ACTION.

Method The teacher asks a student to mime an action. When it is finished, the teacher asks another student: 'What was he/she doing?' The student replies as in the example. If the teacher thinks it necessary, he may first mime an action himself. No student should be allowed to speak until the mime is over.

Example
TEACHER TO STUDENT A: Type a letter.
   (Student A mimes this.)

TEACHER TO STUDENT B: What was he doing?
STUDENT B: He was typing a letter.

●*Drill*
Clean your teeth.
Knit.
Lay the table.
Play the violin.
Wash the dishes.
Make a bed.
Drive a car.
Iron some clothes.
Write a letter.
Make a telephone call (using a public telephone).
Put on a record.
Make some tea/coffee.
Conduct an orchestra.
Thread a needle.
Arrange some flowers.

UNIT 33 *Intermediate*

To *practise the* PAST CONTINUOUS *for a* LONG-LASTING PAST ACTION.

Method The teacher conducts the drill according to the example, requiring the students to use the clues provided. Before beginning, he should explain to the students that, in answer to his first question, they should give a length of time which is *longer than expected*.

Example

TEACHER: How long were you in the shed?
STUDENT: I was in the shed for an hour.
TEACHER: What were you doing all that time?   chop wood
STUDENT: I was chopping wood.

● *Drill*

How long were you in the kitchen?	wash up
How long were you in the attic?	look for my suitcase
How long were you in the office?	type a report
How long were you in the garage?	clean my bicycle
How long were you at the barber's?	wait my turn
How long were you at the airport?	watch the planes
How long were you in the cellar?	get the coal in
How long were you outside the cinema?	queue up
How long were you in the bathroom?	wash my hair
How long were you in the garden?	weed
How long were you in the sitting room?	read
How long were you in the pub?	play darts
How long were you in hospital?	convalesce
How long were you in the library?	choose a book
How long were you on the telephone?	discuss my holiday
How long were you at your friend's house?	listen to records
How long were you in the park?	exercise the dog
How long were you in the store?	look for a carpet

For extra practice, the teacher may provide the cues for the students to ask the questions.

Example

TEACHER: in the shed.
STUDENT A: How long were you in the shed?
STUDENT B: I was in the shed for an hour.
STUDENT A: What were you doing all that time?
STUDENT B: I was chopping wood.

UNIT **34**   *Advanced*

To practise the special use of the PAST CONTINUOUS *with*

always.

Note The use of *always* with the Past Continuous emphasises the unusual (in the opinion of the speaker) frequency of an action in the past. (See Unit 4, p. 4 for similar use of *always* with the Present Continuous.)

Example
TEACHER: He used to tease the dog very often as a child.
STUDENT: He was always teasing the dog as a child.

●*Drill*
He used to make mistakes all the time at school.
They used to have visitors very, very often at their old house.
He used to go to the pictures too much as a boy.
She used to have parties very, very often as a teenager.
He used to argue with me all the time at University.
He used to forget to bring his book very, very often last term.
He used to smile all the time as a little boy.
They used to complain about the government too much in the old days.
She used to change her mind very often in her teens.
They used to quarrel a lot in the early days.
She used to ask for advice very often in the beginning.
He used to talk about television programmes too much at first.
He used to have arguments with his sister very often as a boy.
She used to make silly remarks all the time as a girl.
He used to borrow money too often at University.
She used to tell lies too often as a little girl.
He used to make trouble all the time at college.
He used to interfere with things all the time before his retirement.
She used to grumble about her health all the time before her operation.
He used to bite his nails all the time as a child.
She used to come home after midnight too often as a student.
He used to go up to London very, very often before the war.
I used to bump into him a lot during term time.
She used to buy new clothes very often as a teenager.
He used to get kept in very often at school.
He used to show off all the time at college.
They used to discuss politics all the time at University.
That old radio used to go wrong all the time.
Our previous car used to break down very often.
My last pen used to run out of ink all the time.

UNIT **35** *Intermediate*

To introduce the PAST CONTINUOUS *for* UNFULFILLED

ACTIONS *with Verbs of Anticipation.*

Method   The teacher first writes the following list of Verbs of Anticipation on the blackboard:

> EXPECT
> HOPE
> INTEND
> MEAN
> PLAN

Pointing to an appropriate verb, the teacher asks the question, requiring the students to answer: 'I don't know, but . . .', using the verb in the Past Continuous, as in the example. In all the responses two or more of the verbs can be used. For extra practice the drill may be repeated, varying the verbs.

Example
TEACHER: (pointing to HOPE) Did he go to the party?
STUDENT: I don't know, but he was hoping to.

●*Drill*

Did he buy a bottle of wine?	(intend)
Did she see him yesterday?	(hope)
Did they come last night?	(plan)
Did he phone her yesterday?	(mean)
Did she go to the theatre last week?	(plan)
Did he tidy up the garden?	(intend)
Did he pass the exam?	(expect)
Did she ask him about it?	(mean)
Did they go to Brighton for the weekend?	(hope)
Did she see him at the club on Wednesday?	(expect)
Did she catch the 12 o'clock train?	(plan)
Did they take any photos?	(hope)
Did he write to them last week?	(mean)
Did they get a letter from her last week?	(expect)
Did he have lunch in town?	(plan)

UNIT 36 *Advanced*

To practise the PAST CONTINUOUS *for* UNFULFILLED ACTIONS *with Verbs of Anticipation.*

Part I

Method The teacher first writes the following list of Verbs of Anticipation on the board:

EXPECT
INTEND
HOPE
PLAN

He then asks the question, pointing to an appropriate verb. The students reply, using the verb in the Past Continuous and a suitable Present or Future expression of time, and adding, for the first drill; '. . . but I/he shan't/won't be able to.', and for the second drill: '. . . but I/he shan't/won't have time.', as in the examples. Like the previous drill, Unit 35, these drills may be repeated for extra practice, varying the verbs in brackets.

Example
TEACHER: (pointing to HOPE): When is he going to get a new suit?
STUDENT: Well, he was hoping to next week, but he won't be able to.

● *Drill*

When are they going to move into their new house?	(expect)
When are you going to have a party?	(hope)
When is she taking her exam?	(intend)
When is she going to visit her uncle in hospital?	(plan)
When are you taking the day off?	(hope)
When are they going to put in central heating?	(plan)
When is he going to change his car?	(plan)
When are they going to emigrate to Australia?	(expect)
When are you going to pay back the money?	(intend)
When is she going dancing again?	(hope)
When are they going to have the house painted?	(hope)
When are they going to have the chimney swept?	(plan)
When are they getting married?	(plan)
When are they getting back from their holiday?	(expect)
When is she going to the West Indies?	(plan)

Example
TEACHER (pointing to INTEND): When are you going to get the tickets?
STUDENT: Well, I was intending to tomorrow, but I shan't have time.

●*Drill*

When are you going to mow the lawn?	(plan)
When are you going to pay the bill?	(intend)
When is he going to finish his book?	(hope)
When are you going to have a haircut?	(intend)
When is she going to wash the curtains?	(intend)
When are you going to stick the photos in the album?	(hope)
When is he going to oil the lock?	(intend)
When are you getting your car mended?	(plan)
When is he going to translate the letter?	(intend)
When is she going to do the ironing?	(hope)
When is he leaving for Madrid?	(plan)
When is she going to spring-clean the dining-room?	(plan)
When are you seeing her again?	(expect)
When are you going to listen to your new record?	(hope)
When are they drawing the raffle prizes?	(intend)

Part II

Method The teacher first writes EXPECT and HOPE on the blackboard. He then asks the questions, pointing to whichever he wants used in the answer. The students answer the questions in any suitable way, using the verb indicated in the Past Continuous.

Example
TEACHER (pointing to EXPECT): His wife was out when he came home from work. Why was he annoyed?
STUDENT: Because he was expecting to find his dinner ready.

●*Drill*

Why were you surprised when I came into the room?	(expect)
He got £100 in the will. Why was he disappointed?	(expect)
Why were you disappointed when you heard the exam results?	(hope)
Why did you look pleased when you got the bill?	(expect)
Her husband booked a holiday in France. Why was she annoyed?	(hope)
She came third in the competition. Why was she disappointed?	(hope)
Why did she look angry when the rain started?	(hope)
He offered to lend you £5. Why were you disappointed?	(hope)
The manager is a woman. Why were you surprised?	(expect)
The children were up when you got home. Why were you annoyed?	(expect)
Sixty people came to the meeting. Why was the speaker upset?	(hope)

It was one o'clock when she went to bed. Why was she annoyed? (hope)
He got £5,000 for the house. Why was he displeased? (hope)
They caught the 1.50 train. Why were they annoyed? (expect)
This year's profit was the same as last year's. Why is he
   disappointed? (hope)
Why was she disappointed when she answered the telephone? (expect)
We shall arrive at about 8 o'clock. Why do you keep looking
   at your watch? (hope)
You'll easily finish it tomorrow. Why don't you stop? (hope)
The interview took five minutes. Why was he surprised? (expect)
Why was he annoyed when he received the telephone account? (hope)

UNIT 37 *Advanced*

To practise the PAST CONTINUOUS for UNFULFILLED

ACTIONS.

Note This is a special use of the Past Continuous to indicate that an
original intention has not been fulfilled or has been altered. Special stress
is required. In the sentences presented here, there must always be stress
on the auxiliary verb *was/were* (not on the main verb if this is repeated)
and on whatever other words emphasise the change in plan. Study the
stresses (indicated by italics) in the following:

   (a) He *was* coming on *Thursday*, but *now* he's coming on *Saturday*.
   (b) He *was flying*, but *now* he's coming by *boat*.
   (c) They *were* bringing *two* friends, but *now* they're only bringing *one*.

Method The teacher asks questions about future arrangements. The
students say what each arrangement is now and then go on to mention
what the original (unfulfilled) arrangement was, using the Past Continuous
as in the example. When the students are familiar with the drill they may
be asked to add an explanation, as suggested in brackets.

Example
TEACHER: When is your uncle coming to see you?
STUDENT: He's coming on Saturday. He was coming on Thursday (but
   he can't get away).

   ●*Drill*
   When are you going to the cinema?
   What time are you meeting them?
   When are you seeing her?
   What time are you leaving?
   When is he flying to Paris?
   Which evening are they having the meeting?
   What train are you catching?

When are you taking her to the pictures?
When is he going to (London)?
Who are you bringing to the party?
What are you giving him for his birthday?
When are you writing to her?
How long are you spending there?
When are they moving into their new house?
What are you having for dinner tonight?
Where are you putting your new piano?
How many people are they inviting to the wedding?
What are you giving them to drink?
Which evening are you going to the theatre?
Where are you taking her tonight?
What colour carpet are you getting for the living-room?
Where are they going for their holiday?
How are they going to Istanbul?
What colour are you painting the house?
What car are they getting?

UNIT 38 *Intermediate*

To introduce and practise going to *for an* UNFULFILLED

PAST INTENTION.

Method The students are required to transform the teacher's sentence, as in the example, using one of the expressions below at the end of their sentence:

in the first drill: '. . . but I/he/she/they didn't.'
in the second drill: '. . . but I/he/she/they couldn't.'
in the third drill: '. . . but I/he/she forgot.'

Example
TEACHER: I intended to paint the door cream . . .
STUDENT: I was going to paint the door cream, but I didn't.

● *Drill*
I intended to have a bath.
He intended to change his job.
They intended to play some records.
He intended to grow a beard.
She intended to learn to type.
They intended to get a dog.
They intended to work harder last term.
I intended to invite him to the party.
I intended to send them a wedding present.
They intended to get married last year.

Example
TEACHER: She intended to translate the letter into French . . .
STUDENT: She was going to translate the letter into French, but she couldn't.

● *Drill*
He intended to give up smoking.
I intended to finish it before bed-time.
She intended to fly to Spain.
He intended to take the exam at Christmas.
He intended to build the garage himself.
I intended to save some money.
He intended to catch the 12.30 train.
They intended to sell their house.
She intended to have a party last week.
He intended to get there at three o'clock.

Example
TEACHER: I intended to write it down . . .
STUDENT: I was going to write it down, but I forgot.

● *Drill*
She intended to water the roses.
I intended to take the book back to the library.
She intended to turn off the fire.
He intended to lock the back door.
I intended to ask her about it.
I intended to get him a birthday card.
He intended to telephone his friend.
She intended to tell them about it.
He intended to post the letter.
I intended to book seats.

THE PRESENT PERFECT SIMPLE

To introduce the PRESENT PERFECT SIMPLE, *contrasting*

it with the SIMPLE PAST *by means of actions.*

● *Drill*

(A)

The teacher writes a word on the blackboard, rubs it off, and then says:
> 'I wrote a word on the blackboard.'

The teacher opens the door, closes it, and then says:
> 'I opened the door.'

The teacher closes his book, opens it, and then says:
> 'I closed my book.'

The teacher strikes a match, blows it out, and then says:
> 'I struck a match.'

The teacher turns on the light, turns it off, and then says:
> 'I turned the light on.'

The teacher then repeats the above actions to get responses from the students, asking: 'What did I do?'

The teacher next writes a word on the blackboard and, pointing, says:
> 'I've written a word on the blackboard.'

The teacher opens the door and, pointing, says:
> 'I've opened the door.'

The teacher closes his book and, pointing, says:
> 'I've closed my book.'

The teacher strikes a match, leaves it burning, and, pointing, says:
> 'I've struck a match.'

The teacher turns on the light and, pointing, says:
> 'I've turned the light on.'

The teacher then repeats the above actions to get responses from the students, asking: 'What have I done?'

The teacher then follows the same procedure with each of the following groups of actions to get responses first in the Simple Past and then in the Present Perfect Simple.

(B) I put my pen on the desk.
I took my comb out of my pocket.
I buttoned my jacket.
I made a chalk mark on the wall.
I drew a face on the blackboard.
I took my watch off.

(C) I filled the glass.
I moved the chair near the table.
I raised my right arm.
I shut my eyes.
I gave him a piece of paper.
I pinned the notice on the wall.

UNIT **40** / *Elementary and Intermediate*

To practise the PRESENT PERFECT SIMPLE *to express a*

PRESENT SITUATION.

Method The teacher makes a statement about an action (using the Simple Past) and its present result (using the Present). The students combine the two ideas, using the Present Perfect Simple.

Example
TEACHER: I opened the door and it's open now.
STUDENT: I've opened the door.

●*Drill*
I closed the window and it's closed now.
I put the light on and it's on now.
He went to the barber's and he's there now.
I put the glasses in the cupboard and they're there now.
He took off his jacket and it's off now.
He filled the glass and it's full now.
She turned the radio on and it's on now.
He put the car in the garage and it's there now.
He wiped the blackboard and it's clean now.
She combed her hair and it's tidy now.
She brushed her shoes and so they're clean now.
He broke the window and it's broken now.
He mended the television and it's all right now.

The following examples may be practised with more advanced students.

He went away and he's not back yet.
She laid the table and it's ready now.
She tore her dress and there's a hole in it now.
I wrote three exercises in my book, and here they are.
He repaired his jacket and it's all right now.

He borrowed ten pounds from her and he's still got it.
He forgot her name and he still can't remember it.
He took his car to the garage and it's still there.
She mislaid her pen and she still can't find it.
I paid the bill so I don't owe anything now.
He copied out the answers and they're in his book now.
He put on his coat and he's wearing it now.
He sent his book to the publisher's and they've still got it.
He lost his wallet and he still can't find it.
I hid the money under the tree and it's still there now.

UNIT **41**   *Elementary*

To practise the form of the PRESENT PERFECT SIMPLE

with REGULAR *and* IRREGULAR VERBS.

Note   Part I practises Regular Verbs and Part II practises Irregular Verbs.

Example

   ★Stage One

TEACHER TO STUDENT A:	How many flowers have you picked today?
STUDENT A:	I've picked . . . flowers today.

   Stage Two

TEACHER TO STUDENT B:	Ask A how many flowers he's picked today.
STUDENT B TO STUDENT A:	How many flowers have you picked today?
STUDENT A:	I've picked . . . flowers today.
★TEACHER TO STUDENT B:	What does he say?
STUDENT B:	He says he's picked . . . flowers today.

   Stage Three

TEACHER TO STUDENT B:	Ask him if he's picked (different number) flowers today.
STUDENT B TO STUDENT A:	Have you picked (different number) flowers today?
STUDENT A:	No, I haven't.
★TEACHER TO STUDENT B:	What does he say?
STUDENT B:	He says he hasn't picked (different number) flowers today.

★After a few examples, it should be possible to begin the drill with Stage Two. It should also be possible for the teacher to leave out 'What does he say?' once the students have grasped the form of the drill.

Part I   *Regular Verbs*

●*Drill*

Which month have you booked your holiday in?
What have you cooked for lunch?
Where have you arranged to meet him?
How much money have you saved?
What have you promised to give her?
How many people have you invited to the party?
...re ... planted the flowers?
... ...?
... ...y have you borrowed?
How many questions have you answered?

How many times have you tasted (Chinese) food?
Which countries have you visited?
How many times have you travelled by air?
What languages have you studied?
How many times have you changed your job?
How many schools have you studied in?
How often have you voted?
How many kinds of car have you driven?
How often have you used a typewriter?
How many times have you stayed up all night?

How many times have you watched the television this week?
How often have you telephoned him this week?
How many lessons have you missed this term?
How many days have you attended school this week?
How many letters have you received this week?
How many times have you washed your hair this week?
How many times have you changed your shirt/blouse this week?
How often have you played football/tennis this week?
How many times have you washed up this week?
How often have you listened to the radio this week?

Part II   *Irregular Verbs*

●*Drill*

What have you brought to school with you?
Which books have you left at home?
Where have you put your coat?
What kind of car have you bought?
How many exercises have you written in your book?
What colour have you chosen?
What languages have you learnt?
Where have you hidden the money?
How much money have you lent him?
How many buttons have you sewn on your dress?

Which operas of Mozart have you heard?
How often have you been to (Paris)?
Which plays of Shakespeare have you seen?
What English novels have you read?
How often have you been in hospital?
How many times have you drunk champagne?
How many exams have you taken?
How often have you eaten (spaghetti)?
How many times have you slept outdoors?
How often have you ridden a horse?

How many times have you overslept this term?
How many meals have you eaten today?
How many letters have you written this month?
How many films have you seen this month?
How many cups of coffee have you drunk today?
How much money have you spent this week?
How many times have you caught a cold this year?
How often have you been to the theatre this month?
How many times have you rung up your friend this week?
How many times have you worn your new dress/suit this week?

UNIT **42**   *Elementary*

To contrast the SIMPLE PAST + yesterday, last week, *etc.*

with the PRESENT PERFECT SIMPLE + today, this week, *etc.*

Method The students repeat the teacher's sentence about a past period
of time and then make a similar statement about a present unfinished
period of time, as in the example.

Note Ideally, this drill should be done towards the end of the day, week,
month, etc. The sentence 'She's visited them three times this week'
obviously becomes unrealistic if said on a Monday. The students should
therefore imagine themselves to be speaking at the time appropriate to
each sentence.

Example
TEACHER: She visited them three times last week.
STUDENT: She visited them three times last week.
          She's visited them three times this week.

● *Drill*

She bought three new dresses last week.
He telephoned me twice yesterday.
We did four exercises at school yesterday.
They had two holidays last year.
He took her out three times last week.
She ate three meals yesterday.
He had his hair cut twice last month.
They saw the exhibition twice last year.
There were two big wars last century.
She broke three plates yesterday.
He got good marks in class last week.
I spent fifty pounds last month.
We had two Chinese meals last week.
She smoked twenty cigarettes yesterday.
He borrowed twenty pounds from me last month.
I wrote six letters last week.
They drove a thousand miles last month.
She asked three questions last lesson.
We wasted a lot of time last term.
He was ill four times last year.

UNIT **43**   *Elementary*

To contrast the SIMPLE PRESENT + every day/every week

with the SIMPLE PAST + yesterday/last week *and the*

PRESENT PERFECT SIMPLE + today/this week.

Method The students repeat the teacher's sentence about *every day/every week* and then make similar sentences about *yesterday/last week* and *today/this week*, as in the examples.

Note It is obviously undesirable to do the first drill early in the day, or the second drill early in the week, since many of the sentences would then become unrealistic. (See Note to Unit 42.)

Example
TEACHER: He does five hours work every day.
STUDENT: He does five hours work every day.
          He did five hours work yesterday.
          He's done five hours work today.

●*Drill*

I clean my teeth twice every day.
He does three exercises every day.
We play that record every day.
He drinks three cups of coffee every day.
We walk five miles every day.
She has six telephone calls every day.
I make a lot of mistakes every day.
He smokes ten cigarettes every day.
Our chickens lay a dozen eggs every day.
She types several letters every day.
We drive a hundred miles every day.
He eats two apples every day.
I learn some new words every day.
She teaches three classes every day.
I answer a lot of questions every day.

Example

TEACHER: I watch television twice every week.
STUDENT: I watch television twice every week.
            I watched television twice last week.
            I've watched television twice this week.

●*Drill*

She writes two letters every week.
I spend five pounds every week.
She reads two novels every week.
We waste a lot of time every week.
He visits his friend twice every week.
She has two Chinese meals every week.
He takes that girl out twice every week.
His English improves every week.
I lend her one pound every week.
She cooks the lunch three times every week.
He borrows five pounds from me every week.
He does the washing-up twice every week.
He plays football twice every week.
She finds the lessons difficult every week.
I phone my friend three times every week.

UNIT 44 *Elementary and Intermediate*

To practise the PRESENT PERFECT SIMPLE *after* because.

Method The teacher gives the stimulus, which the students repeat and complete, using *because* and the cues provided, putting the verb into the Present Perfect Simple.

Example
TEACHER: She can't go to the party . . .   catch a cold
STUDENT: She can't go to the party because she's caught a cold.

● *Drill*

I can't see very well . . .	break my glasses
He can't walk very fast . . .	hurt his leg
She can't do the exercise . . .	forget her book
I can't get in . . .	lose my key
I'm walking home . . .	miss the bus
I can't pay the bill . . .	not bring my money
You can't send that letter . . .	write it badly
I can't lend you my dictionary . . .	leave it behind
I know that story very well . . .	see the film
She can drive by herself now . . .	pass her test
I can't post this letter yet . . .	not put a stamp on it
He can't stand up . . .	eat too much
She can't buy any sweets . . .	spend all her money
They can't go on holiday . . .	not save enough
I know him . . .	meet him before

The following may be practised by more advanced students.

We don't know how he is . . .	not hear from him
I'm pleased with myself . . .	work very hard
She can't finish the translation . . .	mislay her dictionary
You can't wear those trousers . . .	not press them
He won't take a cigarette . . .	give up smoking
You can't read the letter . . .	I/post it
They can't get in . . .	she/lock the door
He knows how to do it . . .	I/show him
The teacher's angry with me . . .	I/not do my exercise
I can't tell you the time . . .	my watch/stop
She's very disappointed . . .	he/not telephone
I can't write any more . . .	my pen/run out of ink
I'm going to the police station . . .	someone/steal my bicycle
I don't know the result yet . . .	the post/not come
They don't understand it . . .	the teacher/not explain it

UNIT 45   *Elementary, Intermediate and Advanced*

To practise the PRESENT PERFECT SIMPLE *of Irregular Verbs with* already.

Notes   1. The ideas in Sections A to E practise the past participle forms of most of the Irregular Verbs that students are likely to need. The teacher should make sure that the students have thoroughly mastered the forms in one section before going on to the next. Section F practises verbs with unchanging participle forms, which may be practised at the same time as those in other sections, at the discretion of the teacher.

2. The examples show the two possible positions for *already*: first the usual (pre-participle) position and second the more emphatic (final) position. It is suggested that each section should be practised using *already* (a) in the usual position and (b) in the emphatic position.

Method   The teacher gives the following ideas, requiring the students to answer with the Present Perfect Simple and *already*.

Examples
TEACHER: Bring the milk in, please.
STUDENT: I've already brought it in.

TEACHER: Give him the answer.
STUDENT: I've given it to him already.

Section A   ●*Drill*

> Begin your exercise now.
> When will he come?
> Do your homework.
> You must find those tickets.
> Get your gloves.
> Give him the money.
> When is he going?
> Would you like to hear this record?
> You must keep your promise.
> Make the tea, please.
> You should read this book.
> Say what you want to say.
> Would you like to see my holiday photos?
> Don't sit on that gramophone record.
> He mustn't stand up.
> Take your medicine.
> Tell him the joke.
> Think about it carefully.
> Write the answer.

Section B

Bring it tomorrow.
Buy the tickets.
Drink your tea.
Eat your ice-cream.
Don't fall in love with him/her.
She must feel his pulse.
Don't forget her telephone number.
Are they holding the meeting soon?
You must learn it.
When are you leaving school?
Why don't you light the fire?
You must meet (Mr Robinson).
You must pay him.
Ring the bell.
That pen will soon run out.
Why don't you sell your old car?
You must send that letter today.
Show him how to do it.
Speak to him about it, please.
Why don't you teach him how to swim?
He'll understand soon.

Section C

Don't break the glass.
When are they going to build the wall?
Don't catch my cold.
Please choose the one you want.
Draw the curtains, please.
Would you like to drive his new car?
When are the boxers going to fight?
She'll soon grow tired of him.
You'll lose your boy-/girl-friend.
Would you like to ride my horse?
When is she going to sing?
Why don't you sleep for a little while?
Smell this perfume.
Don't spend that money.
I hope he won't swear.
When is she going to swim the Channel?
You needn't wake him yet.
When is she wearing her new dress?
I think Tom will win the competition.
Wind the clock.

Section D

Is the headmaster going to beat the boy?
It'll become a habit.
Don't bend it.
The guard's going to blow his whistle.
Burn your old love-letters.
I hope you don't dream about it.
When is he flying to Brazil?
You must forgive him.
You ought to hang up your new picture.
You must hide the whisky.
Lay the table, please.
It'll lead to trouble.
Don't lean against the wet paint.
Don't lend him your car.
The moon will soon rise.
They're going to shoot the prisoner.
She'll spell that word wrong.
Be careful or he'll steal it.
Stick the stamp on.
I hope he doesn't tear it.
Throw it away.

Section E

Be careful or that dog will bite you.
Is he creeping up the stairs?
You must deal with that tomorrow.
Dig the hole.
The water will freeze soon.
Feed the chickens.
You must forbid him to see her.
Grind the coffee, please.
Mow the lawn.
Shake the bottle.
It'll shrink if you wash it.
How long will it be before the boat sinks?
Don't let the glass slide down.
Spin the coin.
He mustn't spit here.
Be careful or you'll spoil your dress/suit.
That tiger will spring in a minute.
Sweep the kitchen floor.
The clock will strike in a minute.
Would you sew that button on for me?
Don't tread in the mud.
Be careful or that wasp will sting you.
Don't spill that beer.

Section F

Don't bet on that horse.
I hope your pipes don't burst.
The work will cost a hundred pounds.
Don't cut it.
Don't hit him.
I hope he won't hurt you.
Don't let your house.
Put them away.
You must set your alarm clock.
Shut the door.
The news will soon spread.
Don't upset her.
Don't bid for that vase.
Cast off.
Slit it open.
Split the piece of wood.

UNIT **46**   *Intermediate*

To practise the negative form of the PRESENT PERFECT

SIMPLE *with* since.

Note   *since* = *since the time just mentioned, since that time.*

Method   The teacher gives the first part of the sentence, with the verb
in the Simple Past. The students repeat and add to it, using the same verb
in the Present Perfect Simple negative with *since*.

Example
TEACHER: She saw him two years ago, . . .
STUDENT: She saw him two years ago, but she hasn't seen him since.

● *Drill*
She forgot her book last week, . . .
He came to school last week, . . .
They showed the film last year, . . .
He wrote to his friend last month, . . .
We grew tobacco in 1959, . . .
They chose tomato soup last Sunday, . . .
He took her out last week, . . .
The water froze in 1960, . . .
I drank champagne at the wedding last month, . . .
She did her homework last Wednesday, . . .

We shook the blankets last week, . . .
I woke up at five o'clock last Saturday, . . .
She was here last Monday, . . .
He spoke to them last week, . . .
We ate chicken last weekend, . . .
The car broke down last week, . . .
I flew in his helicopter last month, . . .
She wore her new dress last week, . . .
He blew up his tyre yesterday, . . .
I drove his car two months ago, . . .
She fell over last week, . . .
The price rose last month, . . .
He sang that song last year, . . .
He swam across the river last week, . . .
The dog bit the postman last month, . . .
She swore at him last week, . . .
We rode in his new car last month, . . .
I mowed the lawn last month, . . .
We saw them last week, . . .
She threw the frying-pan at him last week, . . .

UNIT 47 *Elementary*

To practise the PRESENT PERFECT SIMPLE *with* yet.

Method The teacher conducts the drill according to the example, first making it clear that the students must answer the first question in the negative, using *No, I haven't,* etc. or *No, not yet.*

Example

TEACHER TO STUDENT A:	Ask B if he's written anything in his book yet.
STUDENT A TO STUDENT B:	Have you written anything in your book yet?
STUDENT B:	No, I haven't./No, not yet.
TEACHER TO STUDENT A:	What does he say?
STUDENT A:	He says he hasn't written anything in his book yet.

● *Drill*
Have you learnt enough English yet?
Have you seen (name of a film) yet?
Have you finished your exercise yet?
Have you written to your friend yet?
Has she found her handbag yet?
Has he taken her out yet?

Has she cleaned the living-room yet?
Have you got to the end of the book yet?
Has she made the beds yet?
Have you met his girl-friend yet?
Has he translated the book yet?
Has he lost his (French) accent yet?
Have you telephoned your friend yet?
Has she bought the groceries yet?
Has he paid the bill yet?
Has she returned the book yet?
Have you forgiven him yet?
Has she lit the fire yet?
Have they got married yet?
Has she had her baby yet?

UNIT **48** *Elementary*

To practise the PRESENT PERFECT SIMPLE *with*

ever/never.

Method The teacher conducts the drill according to the example, first making it clear that the students must answer the first question in the negative, using *No, I haven't* or *No, never.*

Example
TEACHER TO STUDENT A: Ask B if he's ever had an operation.
STUDENT A TO STUDENT B: Have you ever had an operation?
STUDENT B: No, I haven't./No, never.
TEACHER TO STUDENT A: What does he say?
STUDENT A: He says he's never had an operation.

●*Drill*
Have you ever got drunk?
Have you ever smoked a cigar?
Have you ever eaten caviar?
Have you ever driven a Rolls Royce?
Have you ever been late for school?
Have you ever copied your friend's homework?
Have you ever played in an orchestra?
Have you ever had a car accident?
Have you ever stolen anything?
Have you ever been to Japan?
Have you ever found five pounds in the street?
Have you ever flown in a helicopter?
Have you ever failed an exam?

Have you ever fallen downstairs?
Have you ever broken your leg?
Have you ever told a lie?
Have you ever cheated at cards?
Have you ever forgotten her birthday?
Have you ever overslept?
Have you ever run out of petrol?

UNIT **49**   *Intermediate*

To practise the negative forms of the PRESENT PERFECT

SIMPLE *with* still.

Method The teacher gives the stimulus, which the students repeat and complete, using *still* and the cues provided with the verb, in the Present Perfect Simple negative, as in the example.

Example
TEACHER: She's been in the shop for ages but she . . .   buy anything
STUDENT: She's been in the shop for ages but she still hasn't bought anything.

●*Drill*

I've written to them three times but they . . .	reply
I've asked you again and again but you . . .	do it
She's sent him three letters but he . . .	write back
I lent him ten pounds last month but he . . .	pay me back
I bought ten cigarettes a week ago but I . . .	smoke them all
He borrowed my book last term but he . . .	give it back
He's written to them every weekend but they . . .	answer
She's had that dictionary for a long time but she . . .	use it
I broke my pen ages ago but I . . .	buy another
I gave her five pounds two weeks ago but she . . .	return it
I made this shirt dirty last week but I . . .	wash it
He gave me this record for my birthday but I . . .	play it
I bought this whisky months ago but I . . .	drink it
I finished reading my library books ages ago but I . . .	change them
He broke the window three weeks ago but he . . .	mend it

The following examples may be used if the Present Perfect Continuous has already been practised.

He's been looking for his pen for days but he . . .	find it
She's been waiting for him for ages but he . . .	come home
I've been doing it for three weeks but I . . .	finish it

I've been reading this book for a long time but I . . .	reach the end
She's been trying for weeks but she . . .	succeed
He's been looking for her for ten minutes but he . . .	recognise her
I've been studying this problem for ages but I . . .	get the answer
She's been typing letters all the morning but she . . .	do them all
He's been eating for half an hour but he . . .	have enough
She's been living there for two months but she . . .	pay the rent
The teacher's been explaining it for ages but they . . .	understand
She's been sitting by the fire for an hour but she . . .	get warm
He's been working there for ten years but he . . .	have a rise
She's been practising that song for a week but she . . .	learn it
He's been learning to drive for ages but he . . .	pass his test

---

UNIT 50   *Intermediate*

To contrast the PRESENT PERFECT SIMPLE *with the*

SIMPLE PAST.

Method   The teacher first tells the students that they must answer the first question in each pair in the affirmative. He then conducts the drill as in the example.

Example

Stage One

TEACHER TO STUDENT A:	Ask B if he's written the letter.
STUDENT A TO STUDENT B:	Have you written the letter?
STUDENT B:	Yes, I have.
*TEACHER TO STUDENT A:	What does he say?
STUDENT A:	He says he's written the letter.

Stage Two

TEACHER TO STUDENT A:	Ask him when he wrote the letter.
STUDENT A TO STUDENT B:	When did you write the letter?
STUDENT B:	I wrote it (last night).
*TEACHER TO STUDENT A:	What does he say?
STUDENT A:	He says he wrote it (last night).

*It should be possible to leave out 'What does he say?' after a few examples.

●*Drill*
Have you played your new record?
When did you play your new record?

Have you had breakfast?
When did you have breakfast?

Have you heard the news?
When did you hear the news?

Have you received your money?
When did you receive your money?

Have you pressed/ironed your trousers/dress?
When did you press/iron your trousers/dress?

Has she finished her homework?
When did she finish her homework?

Has he gone to America?
When did he go to America?

Have they seen the film?
When did they see the film?

Have they decided to go abroad?
When did they decide to go abroad?

Has she received your letter?
When did she receive your letter?

Has he started to learn (French)?
When did he start to learn (French)?

Have they paid back the money?
When did they pay back the money?

Has she taken the examination?
When did she take the examination?

Have they returned from (France)?
When did they return from (France)?

Has she found her umbrella yet?
When did she find her umbrella?

Has he got married yet?
When did he get married?

Has she posted the letter yet?
When did she post the letter?

Has he come out of prison yet?
When did he come out of prison?

Have you wound your watch recently?
When did you wind your watch?

Have you been to the cinema recently?
When did you go to the cinema?

Have you watched television lately?
When did you watch television?

Have you travelled by bus lately?
When did you travel by bus?

To practise the PRESENT PERFECT SIMPLE *with* just.

Example
TEACHER: I heard the news on the radio a quarter of an hour ago.
STUDENT: I've just heard the news on the radio.

●*Drill*
I finished that book a short time ago.
He gave up smoking a few days ago.
I remembered her name a few seconds ago.
He recovered from his illness yesterday.
I said good-bye to her a little while ago.
She had a bath an hour ago.
I found those old photographs not so long ago.
He turned the light out a short time ago.
She opened the window a few seconds ago.
I met him again less than an hour ago.
She came to England a day or two ago.
I had this suit cleaned a few days ago.
I explained it to you a few minutes ago.
She telephoned five minutes ago.
I put a cigarette out a second ago.
He began learning English only a week ago.
They got married a few days ago.
I threw it away a few minutes ago.
They bought a house a few weeks ago.
She lost her umbrella a few hours ago.
I passed my driving test a few days ago.
She ate the last one a few seconds ago.
It started to rain a few minutes ago.
The cat had kittens a few days ago.
The milk boiled over a minute ago.

UNIT 52 *Intermediate*

To practise the PRESENT PERFECT SIMPLE *with* only just.

Note The use of *only just* often indicates surprise or impatience, and the students should be encouraged to show these emotions in the responses they make.

Method The teacher makes a statement and the students respond with an exclamation, introducing it with 'But . . .' and using the cue provided (with the verb in the Present Perfect Simple) and *only just*.

Example
TEACHER: She's lost his letter.   receive it
STUDENT: But she's only just received it!

●*Drill*
She's going back home tomorrow.	arrive
My pen's run out again.	fill it
He's going out.	come in
I've mislaid my pen.	buy it
She's smashed her car.	get it
I've got jam on my trousers.	have them cleaned
He's lost my address.	write it down
He's putting on his new record.	play it
He's leaving the club soon.	join
I can't find my pencil.	put it down
He's lighting a cigarette.	put one out
I've broken my glasses.	get them
She's got 'flu.	recover from a cold
My watch has stopped.	wind it
He says he's coming back tomorrow.	go away
She's putting her coat on.	take it off
He says he's hungry.	have a meal
He's spent all his money.	receive it
They're getting married soon.	get engaged
He says he feels tired again.	wake up
Your hair's very untidy.	comb it
Your shoes are dirty.	polish them
They're selling their house.	move in
She's having a holiday next month.	have one

UNIT 53   *Intermediate*

To practise the PRESENT PERFECT SIMPLE *with* for *and*

since.

Section A with *for*

Example
TEACHER: The last time I read the newspaper was ages ago.
STUDENT: I haven't read the newspaper for ages.

● *Drill*
The last time I smoked a cigarette was a week ago.
The last time we gave a party was six months ago.
The last time she spoke French was five years ago.
The last time I changed my shirt was four days ago.
The last time they drank beer was a fortnight ago.
The last time he used an electric razor was two years ago.
The last time he forgot her birthday was five years ago.
The last time we stopped was ages ago.
The last time I made a mistake was three days ago.
The last time he worked late was two months ago.
The last time she polished the furniture was weeks ago.
The last time he taught French was two terms ago.
The last time she said good morning to me was two weeks ago.
The last time she left the house was three days ago.
The last time it rained was three weeks ago.
The last time I thought about her was ages ago.
The last time he did his homework was two weeks ago.
The last time we received a letter was a fortnight ago.
The last time I enjoyed a film was ages ago.
The last time he shaved was three days ago.
The last time I sent a letter to my friend was a fortnight ago.
The last time he saw his brother was ten years ago.

Section B with *since*

Example
TEACHER: The last time I cleaned my teeth was at eight thirty.
STUDENT: I haven't cleaned my teeth since eight thirty.

● *Drill*
The last time I had a glass of champagne was at Christmas.
The last time I ate caviar was on my sister's birthday.
The last time he washed his hands was at breakfast.
The last time I bought any cigarettes was yesterday morning.
The last time she met her cousin was in 19 . . .

The last time I cooked the lunch was in August.
The last time I rode in a sports car was in the summer.
The last time I heard from him was on my birthday.
The last time she put on her fur coat was in the winter.
The last time we looked at our stamp collection was in the spring.
The last time I tried to do that exercise was on Monday.
The last time he missed his train was last Wednesday.
The last time they saw their friends was in 19 . . .
The last time we voted was in 19 . . .
The last time they quarrelled was on his birthday.
The last time she fed the chickens was at nine o'clock.
The last time I wrote a letter to him was in January.
The last time she phoned me was on Tuesday.
The last time they spent a weekend in Paris was in 19 . . .
The last time I answered a question correctly was on Monday.
The last time we travelled by train/air was in 19 . . .
The last time he wore a suit was at the party.
The last time I lent him money was in July.
The last time he played football was in the winter.
The last time he gave me a present was at Christmas.

Section C with *for* and *since*

● *Drill*
The last time we visited our friends was at Easter.
The last time she was here was a year ago.
The last time I drove a car was six months ago.
The last time he spoke to her was at the meeting.
The last time I wound my watch was twenty-four hours ago.
The last time she saw him was at the party.
The last time they borrowed money was in April.
The last time I listened to records was a fortnight ago.
The last time he complained about the weather was on Saturday.
The last time I dreamt about her was ages ago.
The last time she practised the piano was a week ago.
The last time I slept well was at the weekend.
The last time she cooked steak was a month ago.
The last time we swam in the sea was in the summer.
The last time she broke a plate was a week ago.
The last time he paid his rent was two months ago.
The last time I watched television was on Wednesday.
The last time she cut her nails was a fortnight ago.
The last time he pressed his trousers was three weeks ago.
The last time he dug the garden was in the summer.
The last time she helped her mother in the house was a month ago.
The last time she dyed her hair was during her holiday.
The last time the chicken laid an egg was a week ago.
The last time the sun shone was on Thursday.
The last time I hired a car was in August.

UNIT **54**   *Intermediate*

To practise the PRESENT PERFECT *of 'to be' with* for *and*

since *where* have/has been *replaces other verbs in the*

SIMPLE PAST.

Section A with *for*

Example
TEACHER: He became a salesman six months ago.
STUDENT: He's been a salesman for six months.

●*Drill*
He became a doctor ten years ago.
She went on holiday a month ago.
He fell ill three weeks ago.
The weather turned wet three days ago.
She became a nurse five years ago.
He started to be absent three days ago.
We came in a quarter of an hour ago.
He arrived at this school six months ago.
He became a member of parliament several years ago.
The weather turned dull a few days ago.
They got married four years ago.
He went upstairs two hours ago.
It got dark an hour ago.
The workmen went on strike three weeks ago.
The soldier went on duty two hours ago.

Section B with *since*

Example
TEACHER: The television was put on at half past five.
STUDENT: The television's been on since half past five.

●*Drill*
He arrived here on Monday.
She became a teacher in 19 . . .
He fell asleep at two o'clock.
The heating was put on at two o'clock.

We came home at tea-time.
The weather turned cold on Wednesday.
They went away in January.
I got up at half past six.
He became a lawyer in 19 . . .
She went out at four o'clock.
They got busy at the end of November.
Queen Elizabeth II became queen in 1952.
It got foggy yesterday.
He arrived there on Thursday night.
The window got broken last week.

UNIT 55   *Intermediate*

To practise have been *as an extension of the verb 'go'.*

Note   been = *gone and returned.*

Method   The teacher makes a statement about a past period of time,
requiring the students to make a similar statement about the equivalent
present period of time. He should make sure that the times are properly
converted, as follows:

                    yesterday . . . today
                    yesterday morning . . . this morning
                    last week . . . this week
                    last month . . . this month
                    last year . . . this year   etc.

Example
TEACHER: She went to the grocer's twice last week.
STUDENT: She's been to the grocer's twice this week.

●*Drill*
She went to her friend's house yesterday.
He went to the dentist last week.
They went fishing twice last week.
I went to the library last month.
We went to the museum last week.
He went to the swimming-pool twice last month.
They went to the beach twice last week.
She went shopping yesterday morning.
We went to the park three times last week.

He went skating twice last week.
She went to the Chinese restaurant twice last month.
They went hunting three times last year.
She went bathing three times last week.
He went to the barber's twice last month.
We went riding last week.
They went to the Art Gallery twice last year.
She went to the hairdresser's yesterday.
He went shooting three times last season.
They went to the theatre twice last week.
She went to the hospital twice last month.

UNIT **56** *Intermediate*

To practise have been (*as an extension of the verb 'go'*)

with for + *period of time.*

Note been = gone and returned.

Example
TEACHER: It's ages since I went there.
STUDENT: I haven't been there for ages.

●*Drill*
It's three weeks since he went out with her.
It's a long time since I went to (London).
It's a week since she went to school.
It's years since he went to the doctor.
It's two weeks since I went dancing.
It's months since we went to that cinema.
It's a long time since I went abroad.
It's over a fortnight since he went to the barber's.
It's a long time since we went to that restaurant.
It's weeks since I went to a concert.
It's over a week since we went to the pictures.
It's ages since she went to church.
It's days since we went there.
It's over a month since she went out of the house.
It's years since we went away for a holiday.
It's months since I went to a party.
It's days since she went for a ride in his car.
It's over a month since I went to their house.
It's over five years since he went to the Continent for a holiday.
It's ages since I went out with the boys.

THE PRESENT PERFECT CONTINUOUS

UNIT 57   *Intermediate*

To introduce the PRESENT PERFECT CONTINUOUS.

Method The teacher arranges suitable situations and makes comments about them. After presenting all the situations, he repeats each one separately for question and answer, as in the example.

Example

TEACHER: I sat down here a minute ago, and I'm still sitting here.
          I've been sitting here for a minute.

TEACHER: How long have I been sitting here?
STUDENT: You've been sitting there for a minute.

● *Drill*

I opened my book a minute ago, and I'm still looking at it.
I've been looking at my book for a minute.

I picked up my pen two minutes ago, and I'm still writing in my book.
I've been writing in my book for two minutes.

I came over to the window two minutes ago, and I'm still standing here.
I've been standing at the window for two minutes.

I picked up this book five minutes ago, and it's still in my hand.
I've been holding this book for five minutes.

I put this sweet in my mouth a minute ago, and I haven't finished it yet.
I've been sucking this sweet for a minute.

I put on this (shirt) three hours ago, and I'm still wearing it.
I've been wearing this (shirt) for three hours.

I put this photo in my pocket two days ago, and it's still there.
I've been carrying this photo in my pocket for two days.

I started this lesson ten minutes ago, and I'm still teaching you.
I've been teaching you for ten minutes.

I began these examples five minutes ago, and I haven't finished them yet
I've been doing these examples for five minutes.

UNIT 58 *Intermediate*

To practise the PRESENT PERFECT CONTINUOUS *with* for *and* since.

Note These drills should not be attempted until *for* and *since* have been introduced and practised with the simple tense.

Examples
TEACHER: I started to play records an hour ago, and I'm still playing them.
STUDENT: I've been playing records for an hour.

TEACHER: They started working on the project last April, and they're still working on it.
STUDENT: They've been working on the project since last April.

●*Drill*
He started to live in Japan twenty years ago, and he's still living there.
She started to cry about half an hour ago, and she's still crying.
She started to type letters at quarter past nine, and she's still typing them.
They started to learn Arabic two years ago, and they're still learning it.
He started to talk to her about it at three o'clock, and he's still talking.
He started to drink whisky at nine o'clock this morning, and he's still drinking it.
I started to study Algebra in 19 . ., and I'm still studying it.
He started to grow a beard a week ago, and he's still growing it.
They started to eat sandwiches half an hour ago, and they're still doing it.
It started to rain at four o'clock, and it's still raining.
He started fishing in this river at lunchtime, and he's still fishing here.
He started to earn £2,000 a year in 19 . ., and he's still earning it.
He started to write a book at Christmas, and he's still writing it.
They started to smoke cigars at dinner, and they're still smoking.
They started to listen to the radio an hour ago, and they're still doing it.
He started standing in the queue ten minutes ago, and he's still standing there.
He started waiting for the bus at two o'clock, and he's still waiting.
She started resting at three o'clock, and she's still resting.

Examples
TEACHER: I began to decorate this room three days ago, and I haven't finished yet.
STUDENT: I've been decorating this room for three days.

TEACHER: He began cleaning the car at nine o'clock, and he hasn't finished yet.
STUDENT: He's been cleaning the car since nine o'clock.

●*Drill*

I began to write my essay three hours ago, and I haven't finished yet.
I began to clean the silver half an hour ago, and I haven't finished yet.
She began to lay the table at one o'clock, and she hasn't finished·yet.
She began to wash the sheets an hour ago, and she hasn't finished yet.
He began playing the piano at tea-time, and he hasn't finished yet.
We began to do this exercise ten minutes ago, and we haven't finished yet.
She began to cook the meal at quarter past twelve, and she hasn't finished yet.
I began to mow the lawn at half past six, and I haven't finished yet.
She began to polish the table a quarter of an hour ago, and she hasn't finished yet.
He began to translate the book ages ago, and he hasn't finished yet.
He began to prepare his lessons at eight o'clock, and he hasn't finished yet.
He began to read that novel two weeks ago, and he hasn't finished yet.
She began to work at eight o'clock, and she hasn't finished yet.

To express the following ideas, the Present Perfect Continuous is used for constantly Repeated Actions.

Example
TEACHER: He started to help her with her homework months ago, and he still does.
STUDENT: He's been helping her with her homework for months.

●*Drill*

I started to go to the cinema years ago, and I often go there now.
He started to read travel books ages ago, and he still reads them.
He started to shave twice a day in February, and he still does.
She started to buy her clothes in that shop in the spring, and she still buys them there.
I started to send her a Christmas card every year in 19. ., and I still do.
He started to travel to (London) every day ten years ago, and he still does.
She started to do people's hair in 19 . ., and she still does.
He started to mend shoes for a living five years ago, and he still does.
We started to hear from him once a month at the end of the war, and we still do.
They started to pay him by cheque in January, and they still do.
He started to take her out three months ago, and he still does.
She started to write to me every month six months ago, and she still does.
He started to give parties regularly years ago, and he still does.
She started to attend concerts in the autumn, and she still does.
We started to drink that wine on our holiday, and we drink it regularly now.
He started to visit his cousin regularly months ago, and he still does.
I started to do morning exercises years ago, and I still do.
He started to catch the eight-fifteen train every day last spring, and he still does.

UNIT 59   *Intermediate*

To practise the PRESENT PERFECT CONTINUOUS *with* for *and* since.

Note Sections A and B are designed for students who require additional practice of *for* and *since*. With other students it should only be necessary to use Sections C and D.

Section A with *for*

Example
TEACHER: He began wearing those trousers a year ago.
STUDENT: He's been wearing those trousers for a year.

●*Drill*
He began smoking three years ago.
She began living in (England) a year ago.
He began learning the piano six years ago.
I began learning English six months ago.
He began wearing glasses a month ago.
She began going out with him a fortnight ago.
We began collecting stamps ten years ago.
They began travelling to (London) a year ago.
He began growing a beard a week ago.
They began taking French lessons two terms ago.
She began staying in that house six months ago.
They began waiting for you ten minutes ago.
We began going to school a term ago.
He began playing football a year ago.
It began raining half an hour ago.
He began walking to work a month ago.
They began eating Indian food several years ago.
She began driving a car two years ago.
They began arguing about it hours ago.
He began working in that office six months ago.

Section B with *since*

Example
TEACHER: He began studying mathematics in 1962.
STUDENT: He's been studying mathematics since 1962.

●*Drill*
I began waiting for him at five o'clock.
He began teaching that class at Christmas.
She began living here in 19 . . .
He began earning his own living last year.
They began studying English on May 1st.
She began learning the violin in October.
It began raining at four o'clock.
She began typing that letter at four o'clock.
He began wearing that old coat in 19 . . .
They began working in that factory in August.
She began smoking heavily at Christmas.
He began collecting beer-mats on his holiday.
She began using a typewriter on her birthday.
I began reading that book on Monday.
He began lecturing at half past two.
They began playing their gramophone at six o'clock.
She began driving a car last summer.
He began doing that exercise at two o'clock.
She began writing that letter at half past three.
We began going to concerts last autumn.

Section C with *since/ever since* + clause

Example
TEACHER: He began collecting records after he went to his first concert.
STUDENT: He's been collecting records since/ever since he went to his first concert.

●*Drill*
He began biting his nails when he was a little boy.
She began coming in late when she was twenty-one.
He began earning his own living when he left home.
They began working harder when they failed the exam.
He began using after-shave lotion when he met her.
She began living a quiet life when her husband died.
I began listening to the radio after you went out.
She began blushing when he came into the room.
They began living in a larger house when his salary went up.
He began drinking heavily after his wife left him.
He began looking at the television when he turned off the radio.
I began using these batteries after he recommended them.
He began spending a lot of money when he won the football pools.
I began tidying up the room when you went out.
She began eating a lot of sweets when she gave up smoking.

Section D with *for* and *since*

●*Drill*

I began looking for you at lunch-time.
We began shivering when he opened the window.
They began talking about that half an hour ago.
She began practising the piano at four o'clock.
They began building that block of flats two months ago.
She began darning my socks at tea-time.
I began asking him to mend the clock weeks ago.
He began sleeping three hours ago.
She began buying her clothes at that shop when she was sixteen.
They began taking their holidays in July many years ago.
He began getting home at six o'clock when he took his new job.
She began getting ready to go out at half past five.
They began heating their house with oil when the price of electricity
   went up.
It began snowing two days ago.
He began fishing at nine o'clock this morning.
He began snoring when he fell asleep.
She began asking him questions at lunch-time.
We began feeling cold when you turned off the fire.
She began cooking the dinner an hour ago.
She began attending this school at the beginning of the term.
He began trying to undo his shoelace twenty minutes ago.
They began quarrelling when they got married.
I began thinking about that problem days ago.
He began painting the ceiling at the weekend.
She began bathing the baby half an hour ago.

UNIT **60** *Intermediate*

To practise the PRESENT PERFECT CONTINUOUS *with*

for the last . . . *and* since last . . .

Note Before beginning the following drills, compare these sentences:

   (a) I haven't seen him *since last* week/month/year.
   (b) I haven't seen him *for the last* week/month/year.

In sentence (a) *last week*, etc. refers to a point of time in the past and is
therefore used with *since*; in sentence (b) *the last week*, etc. refers to a
period of time continuing up to the present (it is in fact a more emphatic
way of saying (*for*) *a week/month/year*) and is therefore used with *for*. It
may be worth pointing out that in sentence (b), but not in sentence (a),
the word *past* may be used instead of *last*.

Section A   LAST (with *since*)

Method   The teacher requires the students to transform his sentences, using the Present Perfect Continuous with *since* + *last week/month/year.*

Example

TEACHER: He began shaving last year.
STUDENT: He's been shaving since last year.

●*Drill*

She began studying French last year.
He began smoking a pipe last month.
I began driving a car last year.
She began living on her own last week.
He began seeing her last month.
They began staying in that hotel last month.
He began working for his exam last year.
He began growing a moustache last week.
She began going to that dentist last year.
He began collecting records last year.
He began reading that book last week.
He began cooking his own food last month.
He began making plans for his holiday last week.
He began using hair cream last month.
She began earning her own living last year.

Section B   THE LAST (with *for*)

Method   The teacher reminds the students of the significance of introducing *the* before the expressions *last week/month/year*. He then requires them to transform his sentences, using the Present Perfect Continuous with *for* + *the last week/month/year.*

Example

TEACHER: He began shaving a year ago.
STUDENT: He's been shaving for the last year.

●*Drill*

She began studying French a year ago.
He began smoking a pipe a month ago.
I began driving a car a year ago.
She began living on her own a week ago.
He began seeing her a week ago.

They began staying in that hotel a month ago.
He began working for his exam a year ago.
He began growing a moustache a week ago.
She began going to that dentist a year ago.
He began collecting records a year ago.
He began reading that book a week ago.
He began cooking his own food a month ago.
He began making plans for his holiday a week ago.
He began using hair cream a month ago.
She began earning her own living a year ago.

UNIT 61 *Intermediate*

To practise the PRESENT PERFECT CONTINUOUS *with* for

or since.

Note This drill should not be attempted until *for* and *since* have been thoroughly practised.

Method The teacher organises the drill according to the following example, allowing the students to answer using either *for* or *since*.

Example

TEACHER TO STUDENT A:	Ask him how long he's been coming to this school.
STUDENT A TO STUDENT B:	How long have you been coming to this school?
STUDENT B:	I've been coming to this school for a term/since May.
TEACHER TO STUDENT A:	What does he say?
STUDENT A:	He says he's been coming to this school for a term/since May.

● *Drill*
How long have you been living in (England)?
How long has she been using that pen?
How long have I been giving you lessons?
How long have they been collecting stamps?
How long has he been playing the piano?
How long have they been going out together?
How long have you been having lessons with me?
How long has he been staying in that house?
How long have we been sitting in this room?
How long has the artist been painting that picture?
How long have you been studying English?

How long has she been driving a car?
How long have I been teaching you?
How long has he been waiting for his turn?
How long have you been attending this class?
How long has he been learning (French)?
How long have they been writing their exercises?
How long have we been speaking English?
How long has he been preparing for his exam?
How long has she been looking at her book?
How long have they been eating (English) food?
How long has the teacher been correcting the exercises?
How long have I been reading these sentences?
How long have you been wearing those shoes?
How long has he been using an English dictionary?
How long have they been talking to each other?
How long has the maid been laying the table?
How long have we been doing this exercise?
How long have you been listening?
How long have they been waiting at the bus stop?

UNIT **62**   *Intermediate*

To contrast how long *with the* PRESENT PERFECT

CONTINUOUS *and* how many *with the* PRESENT PERFECT

SIMPLE.

Note This drill should not be attempted until *for* and *since* have been thoroughly practised.

Method The teacher asks pairs of questions, as in the example, allowing the students to answer using either *for* or *since*.

Example
TEACHER: How long have you been writing letters?
STUDENT: I've been writing letters for an hour/since three o'clock.
TEACHER: How many letters have you written?
STUDENT: I've written four letters.

●*Drill*

How long has she been drinking coffee?
How many cups of coffee has she drunk?

How long have they been walking?
How many miles have they walked?

How long has she been doing exercises?
How many exercises has she done?

How long have you been learning languages?
How many languages have you learnt?

How long has he been taking photographs?
How many photographs has he taken?

How long has she been buying records?
How many records has she bought?

How long has he been collecting stamps?
How many stamps has he collected?

How long have they been picking apples?
How many apples have they picked?

How long has he been taking out girls?
How many girls has he taken out?

How long has he been painting pictures?
How many pictures has he painted?

How long has he been dancing with her?
How many times has he danced with her?

How long have you been reading that book?
How many pages have you read?

How long have they been making carpets?
How many carpets have they made?

How long has she been knitting pullovers?
How many pullovers has she knitted?

How long has he been giving parties?
How many parties has he given?

How long have they been visiting museums?
How many museums have they visited?

How long has she been typing letters?
How many letters has she typed?

UNIT 63   *Advanced*

To practise the special use of the PRESENT PERFECT

CONTINUOUS.

Note   The Present Perfect Continuous is normally used for an action or habit begun in the past and still continuing at the present time. Sometimes, however, the tense is used for a recent action (no longer continuing) to explain a present result. This special use is normally found in such explanatory sentences as: 'I'm out of breath because I*'ve been running*.' or 'He*'s been working* hard; that's why he's gone to bed early.' It is also commonly found in such questions or exclamations as: 'Who*'s been using* this typewriter?' or 'Someone*'s been cooking* onions.'

Method   The teacher gives the stimulus, requiring a student (Student A in the example) to repeat and expand it using *because* and the cue with the verb in the Present Perfect Continuous. Another student (Student B in the example) then changes the order of the sentence made by Student A, using the expression *that's why.*

Example
TEACHER: My throat's dry . . .   talk too much
STUDENT A: My throat's dry because I've been talking too much.
STUDENT B: I've been talking too much; that's why my throat's dry.

● *Drill*

She's looking very ill . . .	overwork
She speaks French very well . . .	stay in Paris
He's got brown fingers . . .	smoke too much
My neck's stiff . . .	sit in a draught
We've spent all our money . . .	buy presents
The pavements are wet . . .	rain
He's got a black eye . . .	fight
They're feeling very tired . . .	work hard
He looks half asleep . . .	rest
They feel exhausted . . .	travel all day
His back aches . . .	garden
We've got very brown . . .	sunbathe
She's carrying a bowl . . .	feed the chickens
I've got cramp in my legs . . .	sit down too long
Her arm feels stiff . . .	play tennis
You've got indigestion . . .	overeat
He's carrying a hammer and nails . . .	mend the fence
I've got a nasty taste in my mouth . . .	eat onions
He's soaked to the skin . . .	walk in the rain
You've got square eyes . . .	watch television too much

The following examples may be done in the same way, or alternatively as a question and answer drill.

Example

TEACHER: Why's your throat dry?   talk too much
STUDENT: Because I've been talking too much.

●*Drill*

She's got a duster in her hand . . .	polish the table
Her hair's wet . . .	swim
He hasn't got any money . . .	gamble
My feet hurt . . .	walk
He's got his glasses on . . .	read the paper
His breath smells . . .	eat garlic
He's hard up . . .	bet on horses
His trousers are scorched . . .	stand too near the fire
I'm carrying this watering-can . . .	water the garden
His trousers are torn . . .	climb trees
He's looking dreamy . . .	think about his girl-friend
She's got her dressing-gown on . . .	have a bath
I've got white fingers . . .	write with chalk
She's feeling tired . . .	have too many late nights
I've got old clothes on . . .	clean out the attic
She's got flour on her hands . . .	make cakes
He's wearing his overalls . . .	paint the door
His hands are black . . .	get the coal in
He's wearing shorts . . .	play football
He's got oil on his hands . . .	clean his bicycle
I'm sweating . . .	move furniture
He's miserable . . .	take an exam
He's got paint on his trousers . . .	decorate the living room
She's got a camera in her hand . . .	take photographs
She's crying . . .	peel onions

| UNIT **64** | *Advanced* |

To practise the special use of the PRESENT PERFECT

CONTINUOUS.

Method   The teacher asks the students to comment on an imaginary situation, using the verbs provided in the Present Perfect Continuous, as in the example.

Example

TEACHER: What might you say if you found that your scissors   use
didn't cut properly?

STUDENT: Someone's been using my scissors.
or
Who's been using my scissors?

● *Drill*

What might you say if you found that your new box   eat
of chocolates was almost empty?

What might you say if you found that the nib of your   write with
pen was bent?

What might you say if you found that your new tube   use
of tooth-paste was half empty?

What might you say if you found that the blade in   shave with
your razor was blunt?

What might you say if you found that half your new   drink
bottle of whisky had gone?

What might you say if you found that your record-   fiddle with
player didn't work properly?

What might you say if you found that the pocket of   wear
your jacket was torn?

What might you say if you found that one of your   play
records was scratched?

What might you say if you found that the pages of   read
one of your books had been marked?

What might you say if you found that the eiderdown   lie
on your bed was crumpled?

What might you say if you found that your photo-   look at
graphs were covered with fingermarks?

What might you say if you found that the ashtray   smoke
was full of cigarette-ends?

What might you say if you found that the papers on   disturb
your desk were all mixed up?

What might you say if you found that your bedroom   tidy
was tidier than it was when you left it?

What might you say if you found that your radio wouldn't work properly?	tamper with
What might you say if you found that there were shoe marks on the table?	stand on
What might you say if you went into a room and found a lot of dirty glasses all over the place?	have a party
What might you say if you went into a room and saw a lot of gramophone records lying about?	listen to
What might you say if you found that one of your records wasn't in its usual place?	mess about with
What might you say if you felt in your pockets and found that your cigarettes had gone?	go through

---

UNIT 65   *Intermediate*

To provide practice in answering questions in the
SIMPLE PAST *and the* PRESENT PERFECT (*Simple and*
Continuous).

Note In reply to questions not beginning with a Question-Word (i.e. *When, What, How,* etc.), the teacher should require the students to give the natural short answer (i.e. 'Yes, he did', 'No, I haven't', etc.) wherever possible.

●*Drill*
How long have you been living in (England)?
How many times have you been to (London)?
Have you ever read ('War and Peace')?
Did you go to the cinema last night?
When did she arrive in . . .?
Has he finished writing his new book yet?
What time did you finish your homework last night?
How long have they been waiting?
Did they telephone or send a letter?
Have you been to the theatre lately?
What time did you leave the house this morning?
How long has she been studying English?
Did he take her out last night?
Where did he take her last week?
How many times have they invited you to their house?
Has he done the exercise yet?
Did she get up early or late yesterday?
How long have we been doing this exercise?
When did you last visit her?
How long have you known him?
When did she have her last accident?

How long has he been trying to give up smoking?
Have you seen her lately?
When did he grow his beard?
Did you find your book in the case or in the drawer?
How many of those chocolates has she eaten?
How long has she been wearing glasses?
When did you buy that dress/tie?
Have they shown you their holiday photographs?
Did he buy a paper yesterday?
How many times has she phoned them this week?
How long have you been using that pen?
How much money did the thief steal?
Have you ever tried to learn (Chinese)?
How many answers did he get right?
Has she been working hard recently?
Did he pass the exam or fail it?
How long have they been writing that exercise?
How many miles did they drive during their holiday?
How many miles has he driven in his new car?
Have you written your exercise in ink or in pencil?
What time did they meet last night?
How long has she been having typing lessons?
What did you do last night?
Have you given her book back yet?
Did you lend him the money or not?
What have they been doing today?
How many presents did you get for your birthday?
Have you brought your raincoat with you today, or have you
    left it at home?
What have we been doing for the last ten minutes?

THE PAST PERFECT SIMPLE

To introduce the PAST PERFECT SIMPLE *by means of*

action chains.

Method The teacher performs the series of actions in group A, commenting as instructed. He then repeats the actions for the students to make the comments: 'After you'd . . ., you. . . .' The same procedure is followed for the other groups.

● *Drill*

(A)

He comes into the room.	
He closes the door.	After I'd come into the room, I closed the door.
He walks to the table.	After I'd closed the door, I walked to the table.
He puts his books down.	After I'd walked to the table, I put my books down.
He pulls out the chair.	After I'd put my books down, I pulled out the chair.
He sits down.	After I'd pulled out the chair, I sat down.
He picks up a book.	After I'd sat down, I picked up a book.
He opens it.	After I'd picked up the book, I opened it.
He starts reading.	After I'd opened the book, I started reading.

(B)

He writes a word on the board	
He picks up the duster.	After I'd written a word on the board, I picked up the duster.
He wipes the board.	After I'd picked up the duster, I wiped the board.
He walks to the window.	After I'd wiped the board, I walked to the window.
He opens the window.	After I'd walked to the window, I opened it.
He shakes the duster out of the window.	After I'd opened the window, I shook the duster.
He closes the window.	After I'd shaken the duster, I closed the window.

He walks back to his desk.	After I'd closed the window, I walked back to the desk.
He puts the duster down.	After I'd walked back to the desk, I put the duster down.

(C)
He sits down.

He opens his writing pad.	After I'd sat down, I opened my writing pad.
He picks up his pen.	After I'd opened my writing pad, I picked up my pen.
He writes a short note.	After I'd picked up my pen, I wrote a short note.
He takes out an envelope.	After I'd written a short note, I took out an envelope.
He writes an address on it.	After I'd taken out an envelope, I wrote an address on it.
He puts the letter in the envelope.	After I'd written the address, I put the letter in the envelope.
He seals the envelope.	After I'd put the letter in the envelope, I sealed it.
He sticks a stamp on it.	After I'd sealed the envelope, I stuck a stamp on it.

Smoking provides particularly good examples of this pattern. If it is allowed in the classroom, the following actions may also be organised.

(D)
He takes out a packet of cigarettes.

He opens it.	After I'd taken out a packet of cigarettes, I opened it.
He takes out a cigarette.	After I'd opened the packet, I took a cigarette.
He picks up a box of matches.	After I'd taken a cigarette, I picked up a box of matches.
He strikes a match.	After I'd picked up the box of matches, I struck one.
He lights the cigarette.	After I'd struck the match, I lit the cigarette.
He blows out the match.	After I'd lit the cigarette, I blew out the match.
He throws it in the waste-paper basket.	After I'd blown out the match, I threw it in the waste-paper basket.
He puts the packet away.	After I'd thrown the match in the waste-paper basket, I put the packet away.
He smokes the cigarette.	After I'd put the packet away, I smoked the cigarette.
He puts it out in the ashtray.	After I'd smoked the cigarette, I put it out in the ashtray.

UNIT **67**   *Intermediate*

To practise the PAST PERFECT SIMPLE *with* after, when

and as soon as.

Method The teacher conducts the drill according to the following example, requiring the students to answer using the cues provided. He should make sure that the students use contracted forms throughout.

Example

TEACHER TO STUDENT A:	Ask B what he did after he'd woken up.	get out of bed
STUDENT A TO STUDENT B:	What did you do after you'd woken up.	
STUDENT B:	I got out of bed.	
TEACHER TO STUDENT A:	Ask him when he got out of bed.	
STUDENT A TO STUDENT B:	When did you get out of bed?	
STUDENT B:	After I'd woken up.	

●*Drill*

What did you do after you'd got up?	wash
What did you do after you'd washed?	clean my teeth
What did you do after you'd cleaned your teeth?	comb my hair
What did you do after you'd combed your hair?	dress
What did you do as soon as you'd dressed?	make my bed
What did you do after you'd made your bed?	come downstairs
What did you do after you'd come downstairs?	eat my breakfast
What did you do after you'd eaten your breakfast?	read the paper
What did you do when you'd read the paper?	put on my coat
What did you do as soon as you'd put on your coat?	come to school
What did you do after you'd got home yesterday?	take off my coat
What did you do as soon as you'd taken off your coat?	have a meal
What did you do when you'd had a meal?	get out my books
What did you do after you'd got out your books?	do my homework
What did you do as soon as you'd done your homework?	put away my books
What did you do after you'd put away your books?	watch television
What did you do when you'd watched television?	go upstairs
What did you do when you'd gone upstairs?	undress
What did you do after you'd undressed?	have a bath
What did you do as soon as you'd had a bath?	go to bed

It is possible for the teacher to build up a drill with the students giving their own ideas, as follows:

TEACHER TO STUDENT A:	Ask B what he did last night.
STUDENT A TO STUDENT B:	What did you do last night?
STUDENT B TO STUDENT A:	I went to the cinema last night.
TEACHER TO STUDENT A:	What does he say?
STUDENT A:	He says he went to the cinema last night.
TEACHER TO STUDENT A:	Ask him what he did when he'd come out of the cinema.
STUDENT A TO STUDENT B:	What did you do when you'd come out of the cinema?
STUDENT B TO STUDENT A:	When I'd come out of the cinema, I went to John's house.
TEACHER TO STUDENT A:	What does he say?
STUDENT A:	He says that when he'd come out of the cinema, he went to John's house.

UNIT 68 *Intermediate*

To practise the PAST PERFECT SIMPLE *with* after, when *and* as soon as.

Method The teacher requires the students to change the sentences, using *after*, *when* and/or *as soon as*. The drill may be repeated several times, (a) using each word in turn throughout the drill and finally mixing them (as suggested by the words in brackets); (b) changing the order of the sentences as shown in the two examples.

Example
TEACHER: She cleaned her teeth and then she had a drink of water. (after)
STUDENT: After she'd cleaned her teeth, she had a drink of water.
   (or) She had a drink of water after she'd cleaned her teeth.

● *Drill*

I finished my breakfast and then I went out.	(when)
He ate all the chocolates and then he was sick.	(as soon as)
She saved up enough money and then she bought the dress.	(when)
He locked the front door and then he went up to bed.	(after)
We decorated the house and then we sold it.	(when)
The train stopped and then we got out.	(as soon as)
I mowed the lawn and then I went in to tea.	(after)
She did her homework and then she watched the television.	(when)
He drank his coffee and then he lit a cigarette.	(as soon as)
We walked six miles and then we sat down for a rest.	(after)
He learnt to dance and then he took her out.	(when)
She studied French and then she went to France.	(as soon as)
She got back home and then she made a cup of tea.	(after)
He won the competition and then he bought a car.	(after)

She put the children to bed and then she started to cook
the supper.   (when)
We arrived at the station and then we bought the tickets.   (as soon as)
He said good night to her and then he drove home.   (when)
He brought in the coal and then he washed his hands.   (after)
The teacher came into the room and then the students
sat down.   (when)
She turned off the electric fire and then she felt cold.   (as soon as)

UNIT 69   *Intermediate*

To practise the PAST PERFECT SIMPLE *with* after.

Method   The teacher says a sentence and then gives a cue. The students
repeat the sentence and expand it with a clause introduced by *after*, using
the Past Perfect Simple of the verb already used, and the cue.

Example
TEACHER: He drank some tea.   lemonade
STUDENT: He drank some tea after he'd drunk some lemonade.

● *Drill*

He ate the apple.	the orange
She wrote him a letter.	a postcard
He showed me the photo.	the book
I tore up the envelope.	the letter
He saw him.	his wife
I did my homework.	the washing-up
We drove to London.	Oxford
She rang up the doctor.	the hospital
They flew to Chicago.	New York
She chose some gloves.	shoes
They sank the submarine.	the battleship
The thief stole the silver.	the jewellery
He rode on a train.	a bus
She spoke in German.	French
I broke the cup.	the saucer
He took off his socks.	his tie
They blew up the Town Hall.	the railway station
The dog bit the postman.	the policeman
He drew the curtains.	the blinds
She threw away the box.	the paper
He woke his mother.	his father
I beat John at tennis.	Tom
He fell in love with Mary.	Betty

UNIT 70   *Intermediate*

To practise the PAST PERFECT SIMPLE *with* because.

Method   The teacher states two facts, the second being a result of the
first. The student reverses them and joins them with *because*, using the
Past Perfect Simple in the second part.

Example

TEACHER: He ate too much chocolate. He was sick.
STUDENT: He was sick because he'd eaten too much chocolate.

● *Drill*

She caught a cold. She couldn't go to the party.
I wrote untidily. The teacher couldn't read my homework.
He forgot to post the letter. She was angry with him.
He drank too much at the party. He woke up with a hangover.
She used a dictionary. She did a perfect exercise.
I left my sunglasses at home. I got a headache.
He didn't sign the cheque. The bank wouldn't pay the money.
She forgot to wind her watch. She missed her train.
He ate his meal too fast. He had indigestion.
She went out without a coat. She caught a cold.
He didn't do his homework. The teacher was annoyed with him.
She lost her key. She couldn't open the door.
She read the book. She knew the story well.
He passed his driving test. He was able to drive by himself.
I fell over. My leg hurt.
He was rude to her. She wouldn't speak to him.
He spilt the gravy. The table-cloth was dirty.
His pen ran out. He couldn't write anything.
They didn't fill up with petrol. The car stopped.
He remembered her birthday. She was pleased.
We didn't eat any breakfast. We felt hungry.
They forgot their money. They couldn't pay the bill.
She saw him at a party. She recognised him.
He didn't understand the question. He gave the wrong answer.
They left the window open. The room was cold.
She left the meeting early. She managed to catch the bus.
He missed the party. He was disappointed.

His wife left him. He was lonely.
I didn't write it down. I forgot the meaning of the word.
They lost their way. They arrived late.
I spent all my money. I couldn't buy any cigarettes.
She didn't sleep all night. She felt very tired.
She locked the door. We couldn't get in.
He smashed up his car. He had to walk to work.
She lost her purse. She went to the police station.
They didn't save enough money. They couldn't go on holiday.
He hurt his back. He couldn't bend down.
His electric razor went wrong. He couldn't shave.
I arrived late. I was punished.
He received many letters of congratulations. He felt very happy.

UNIT 71   *Intermediate*

To practise the PAST PERFECT SIMPLE *with* already.

Example
TEACHER: Why didn't she lock the door?
STUDENT: Because someone had already locked it.

●*Drill*
Why didn't he open the door?
Why didn't she cut the grass?
Why didn't she lay the table?
Why didn't he clean the car?
Why didn't he post the parcel?
Why didn't you the clear the table?
Why didn't he close the window?
Why didn't he empty the ashtray?
Why didn't she make the beds?
Why didn't he light the fire?
Why didn't she tidy the dining room?
Why didn't you pull the curtains?
Why didn't she sweep the floor?
Why didn't she dust the room?
Why didn't you make the tea?
Why didn't she wake him?
Why didn't he take the letters?
Why didn't you ask that question?
Why didn't she polish the piano?
Why didn't he shut the gate?

UNIT 72 *Intermediate*

To practise the PAST PERFECT SIMPLE *with* already

followed by a when-*clause.*

Example
TEACHER: They laid the table and then we arrived.
STUDENT: They'd already laid the table when we arrived.
   (or) When we arrived, they'd already laid the table.

●*Drill*
I sent her three post-cards and then I wrote that letter.
They prepared our rooms and then we arrived.
The old man died and then the doctor got there.
They had three games of cards and then Bill came in.
The car bumped into two trees and then it hit the wall.
I did it and then she asked me.
His wife cooked the lunch and then he got home.
The sun set and then we left.
The concert started and then they arrived.
The student took the exam three times and then he came to
   this school.
Mary put the food on the table and then I came in.
He wrote six novels and then he wrote his autobiography.
They decorated the room and then they moved in.
They finished all the sandwiches and then we arrived.
They had lunch and then we called to see them.

UNIT 73 *Intermediate*

To practise the PAST PERFECT SIMPLE *with* by the time

and the SIMPLE PAST.

Example
TEACHER: He did all his work. He went to bed.
STUDENT: He'd done all his work by the time he went to bed.
   (or) By the time he went to bed, he'd done all his work.

●*Drill*
We got everything ready. They arrived.
The sun set. We left.
He spent all his money. He got home.
They bought all their furniture. They got married.

The secretary typed three letters. I came in.
The telephone stopped ringing. I got downstairs.
The film started. We got into our seats.
He passed all his exams. He left school.
The rain stopped. We were ready to leave.
We did five exercises. The bell rang.
They all went to sleep. The lecture finished.
The fire did a lot of damage. They put it out.
He forgot her name. He got home.
She cooked his breakfast. He came downstairs.
He made a fortune. He became Prime Minister.

UNIT 74   *Intermediate*

To practise the PAST PERFECT SIMPLE *after* REPORTING VERBS *in the* PAST.

Method   The teacher makes a statement about something that happened in the past; then he says that he told someone about this. The students combine the two statements, using a reporting verb (*told*, etc.) in the Simple Past with the second verb in the Past Perfect Simple.

Note   In the first drill the verb *told* is used throughout. In the second drill several different reporting verbs are used.

Example
TEACHER: I did it . . . and afterwards I told her.
STUDENT: I told her that I'd done it.

●*Drill*
We wrote to her . . . and afterwards we told her sister.
They smoked all his cigarettes . . . and afterwards they told him.
She bought a new dress . . . and afterwards she told her friend.
We gave him the money . . . and afterwards we told his brother.
I did my homework . . . and afterwards I told the teacher.
She spoke to him . . . and afterwards she told us.
I fell in love with her . . . and afterwards I told them.
He took the money . . . and afterwards he told the police.
She drank all his whisky . . . and afterwards she told him.
He sent the telegram . . . and afterwards he told his sister.

Example
TEACHER: She broke the teapot . . . and afterwards she admitted it.
STUDENT: She admitted that she'd broken the teapot.

●*Drill*
He stole the papers . . . and afterwards he admitted it.
I hid the money . . . and afterwards I explained.
They made an important discovery . . . and afterwards they announced this.
He arrived . . . and afterwards I mentioned it.
I was rude to her . . . and afterwards she complained.
She found his watch . . . and afterwards she informed him.
He lost the money . . . and afterwards he admitted it.
I read the book . . . and afterwards I told my teacher.
He tore his trousers . . . and afterwards he confessed.
I visited her . . . and afterwards I mentioned this.
He was dismissed from his post . . . and afterwards they announced this.
He ate her last chocolate . . . and afterwards she complained.
I began the work . . . and afterwards I informed the manager.
He chose the dearest seats . . . and afterwards he boasted about it.
We saw the film . . . and afterwards we mentioned this.
The dog bit her . . . and afterwards she complained.
He won the competition . . . and afterwards they let him know.
I forgot to do it . . . and afterwards I admitted it.

UNIT **75**   *Intermediate*

To practise the PAST PERFECT SIMPLE *with only followed*

by when *and the* SIMPLE PAST.

Method   Before beginning the drill, the teacher should point out that the
ideas all have the meaning *less than expected,* and he should make sure
that the students produce the correct stress and intonation to convey this
meaning. He then conducts the drill according to the following example.

Example
TEACHER: I was there for five minutes. John walked in.
STUDENT: I'd only been there for five minutes when John walked in.

●*Drill*
He wore the jacket three times. He gave it away.
We were on holiday a week. We had to return home.
She swallowed three mouthfuls. She felt sick.
We drove five miles. We ran out of petrol.
I was back at work for three days. I caught flu.
She read one page. He took the book away.
We were in the coffee bar for five minutes. Our friends came in.
He used his electric razor three times. It went wrong.

I wrote six lines. My pen ran out of ink.
He read one sentence. I told him to stop.
They walked a hundred yards. They sat down for a rest.
He did half the exercise. He stopped working.
We were in our seats for two minutes. The film started.
He drove fifty yards. The police stopped him.
I was there for five minutes. She arrived.
She was in hospital for a week. She died.
He had three driving lessons. He took his test.
She wrote half the exercise. She went to bed.
I was in the house for a minute. The phone rang.
He had the pen for a week. He lost it.

UNIT 76 *Intermediate*

To practise the PAST PERFECT SIMPLE *with* before *and*

the SIMPLE PAST.

Method Before beginning the drill, the teacher should point out that the ideas all have the meaning *more than expected* and he should make sure that the students produce the correct stress and intonation to convey this meaning. He then conducts the drill according to the following example.

Example
TEACHER: He answered eight advertisements. Then he got a job.
STUDENT: He'd answered eight advertisements before he got a job.

●*Drill*
His wife tried on ten hats. Then she bought one.
We drove more than thirty miles. Then we came to a garage.
He lost five hundred pounds. Then he stopped gambling.
She sat for the exam five times. Then she passed.
They drove a hundred miles. Then they stopped for lunch.
He spent ten pounds. Then he decided to stop.
I wrote him three letters. Then he wrote back.
He danced with her three times. Then he asked her for a date.
We walked ten miles. Then we stopped for a rest.
I took my driving test four times. Then I got through.
The burglar broke into ten houses. Then the police caught him.
He consulted three different doctors. Then he was satisfied.
The teacher asked the same question three times. Then he got an answer.
They ran six miles. Then they began to feel tired.
He tried to telephone her three times. Then he got through.
She tried five different recipes. Then she found one her husband liked.
They lived in many countries. Then they settled in Australia.
The men were on strike for eight weeks. Then an agreement was reached.

UNIT 77　　　　　　　　　　　　　　　　　　　　*Intermediate*

To practise the use of when *and* before *with the* SIMPLE
PAST *and the use of the* PAST PERFECT SIMPLE.

Method　The teacher first explains that he is going to ask questions with
a *when*-clause in the second part, and that he wants the students to answer
using time phrases (with *for*) that imply a length of time which is normal
or expected (as in Example 1). When the questions have been answered in
this way, the teacher explains that he is now going to ask the same
questions with *before* instead of *when* in the second part, and that he wants
the students to answer with time phrases that imply a length of time
which is longer than expected (as in Example 2). He should also draw
the students' attention to the special stress and intonation required with
the second type of time phrase in order to bring out the meaning *lónger
than expected.*

Example 1
TEACHER :　How long had you been in the coffee bar when your friends
　　　　　arrived?
STUDENT :　I'd been in the coffee bar for five minutes when my friends
　　　　　arrived.
　　(or)　When my friends arrived, I'd been in the coffee bar for five
　　　　　minutes.

Example 2
TEACHER :　How long had you been in the coffee bar before your friends
　　　　　arrived?
STUDENT :　I'd been in the coffee bar for nearly an hour before my friends
　　　　　arrived.

●*Drill*
How long had you been on the platform when the train came in?
How long had you been in the queue when you got to the counter?
How long had you been there when David saw you?
How long had you been in the airport when your flight was announced?
How long had you been in the waiting room when the nurse called you?
How long had you been in the dining room when she brought the lunch?
How long had you been outside the cinema when your friends arrived?
How long had they been in the restaurant when the waiter took their
　order?
How long had she been in the shop when she got served?
How long had you been at the bus stop when the bus came?
How long had they been outside the door when he opened it?
How long had you been at the party when your friend arrived?
How long had he been dead when they found him?
How long had he been in prison when he was released?

UNIT **78**   *Intermediate*

To introduce, by means of actions, the PAST PERFECT
SIMPLE *after* before *to indicate that an action was*
prevented or stopped before it was completed.

Method   The teacher does or organises the actions in group A, commenting on each one as instructed. The actions are then repeated for the students to make the comments. The same procedure is followed for groups B and C.

● *Drill*

(A)

He lights a cigarette, smokes it for a short time and then puts it out, remarking:
> 'I put out the cigarette before I'd finished it.'

He tells a student to read a paragraph from a book, but while the student is reading, he closes the book, remarking:
> 'I shut your book before you'd finished reading.'

He offers a student a sweet and, just as the student is about to take one, he snatches the packet away, remarking:
> 'I took the packet away before you'd taken a sweet.'

He writes a sentence on the blackboard, tells the students to copy it in their exercise books but rubs it off before they have had time to do so, remarking:
> 'I wiped the blackboard before you'd finished copying the
> sentence.'

(B)

He tells a student to copy a sentence from a textbook and takes his pen away while he is doing so, remarking:
> 'I took away your pen before you'd finished writing the
> sentence.'

He tells a student to switch on the light, but while he is going to the light switch, he tells him to open the window, remarking:
> 'I told him to open the window before he'd switched on the
> light.'

He gives a student a folded newspaper and tells him to read out the main headline. While the student is unfolding the paper, the teacher tells him what the headline is. Then he says:
'I told you the headline before you'd unfolded the paper.'

He tells a student to come to the blackboard and find the answer to a sum, (e.g. multiplication). While the student is working it out, the teacher writes up his previously prepared version on the other side of the board, remarking:
'I got the answer before you'd finished.'

(C)

He tells a student to go out of the room, but just as the student is opening the door, he tells him to come back, remarking:
'I called him back before he'd left the room.'

He gives a student a glass of water but takes it away just as he is about to drink it, remarking:
'I took away the water before you'd started drinking.'

He tells a student to explain how to get to a certain place. While he is talking, the teacher goes out of the room, remarking on his return:
'I went out of the room before you'd finished explaining.'

He tells a student to read a page of a textbook, but while he is reading it, the teacher turns over the page, remarking:
'I turned over the page before you'd got to the end.'

UNIT **79**   *Intermediate and Advanced*

To practise the PAST PERFECT SIMPLE *after* before *to*

indicate that an action was prevented or stopped before

it was completed.

Part I

Method   The teacher gives two sentences which the students combine, using *before* as in the example.

Example

TEACHER: They left. I hadn't explained properly.
STUDENT: They left before I'd explained properly.

● *Drill*

He arrived. I hadn't finished my lunch.
The children left the class. The bell hadn't rung.
He offered me a drink. I hadn't taken off my coat.
He wanted to go. The lesson hadn't finished.
He asked to borrow the book. I hadn't read it myself.
He went back to work. He hadn't recovered properly.
We managed to arrive at the hall. The concert hadn't started.
He said he didn't like it. He hadn't looked at it.
Her husband died. They hadn't been married six months.
He lost his lighter. He hadn't had it three weeks.
It started to rain. We hadn't reached the end of the road.
They left the table. They hadn't had their coffee.
He laughed. He hadn't heard the end of the story.
John called to see me. I hadn't had breakfast.
We reached the football ground. The game hadn't started.
I got to the station. The train hadn't arrived.
She married him. She hadn't known him three weeks.
The waiter took their plates away. They hadn't finished eating.

The following may also be practised with more advanced students.

The telephone operator cut them off. They hadn't finished their conversation.
She wanted to study for the Proficiency examination. She hadn't taken the Lower Certificate.
He decided to go ahead with his plans. He hadn't received official approval.
The exhibition closed. We hadn't had a chance to see all the pictures.
He gave up smoking. It hadn't got a hold on him.
The climbers called off the climb. They hadn't reached the summit.
He took a dislike to her. He hadn't even set eyes on her.
She served the sweet. We hadn't finished our main course.

Part II

Method The teacher gives a sentence which the students transform, using *before* as in the example.

Example
TEACHER: I hadn't done half the work when he came in.
STUDENT: He came in before I'd done half the work.

● *Drill*
They hadn't got half-way there when the car broke down.
He hadn't swallowed three mouthfuls when he felt sick.
We hadn't driven ten miles when we had an accident.
She hadn't smoked half the cigarette when she started to cough.
They hadn't finished their lunch when he telephoned.
He hadn't mown half the lawn when it began to rain.
I hadn't had a chance to sit down when my friends arrived.
He hadn't opened the safe when the alarm rang.
She hadn't been in bed ten minutes when she fell asleep.
He hadn't been there a week when he left.
They hadn't finished their meal when they left the table.
He hadn't completed his work when he became ill.
She hadn't read a dozen pages when she put the book down.
I hadn't written six lines when my pen ran out.
He hadn't said half a dozen words when she began to laugh.
She hadn't been in the school for a week when she moved to a higher class.

The following may also be practised with more advanced students.

The crew hadn't lowered the boats when the ship sank.
The painter hadn't finished the picture when the collector made an offer.
He hadn't disposed of the stolen jewellery when the police caught him.
He hadn't achieved his ambition when he died.
They hadn't completed the expedition when their supplies ran out.
He hadn't prepared the soil properly when he planted the bulbs.
He hadn't calculated the cost when he undertook to finance the scheme.
They hadn't tested the apparatus when they connected the electricity supply.
He hadn't taken proper aim when he opened fire.
The architect hadn't approved the plans when they started building.

UNIT **80**   *Intermediate and Advanced*

To practise the PAST PERFECT SIMPLE *after* until.

Part I Intermediate

Example
TEACHER: She only noticed it after he'd pointed it out.
STUDENT: She didn't notice it until he'd pointed it out.

●*Drill*
I only went to bed when I'd finished my work.
They only visited him when they'd heard of his illness.
He only began the lesson when all the students had arrived.
I only realised what he meant when I'd put the phone down.
We only left when all the other guests had gone.
I only felt better after I'd had a drink.
He only stopped smoking after the doctor had advised him to.
She only understood the question after he'd changed the words.
The students only stopped talking after the teacher had come in.
He only agreed to do it after they'd asked him three times.
He only gave up gambling when he's lost all his money.
I only enjoyed my tea after I'd put in more sugar.
He only wrote back after she'd written him four letters.
He only signed the paper after he'd read it carefully.
They only came after I'd called three times.

Example
TEACHER: I explained. Then he understood.
STUDENT: He didn't understand until I'd explained.

●*Drill*
She turned off the light. Then he went to sleep.
I offered him a lot of money. Then he promised to do it.
He left. Then I realised my mistake.
He took her out six times. Then she began to like him.
He spent all his money. Then he came home.
She corrected all the mistakes. Then she handed in the essay.
He compared them three times. Then he noticed the difference.
He examined the goods carefully. Then he made out the cheque.
We asked her three times. Then she agreed to do it.
He drove ten miles out of his way. Then he realised he'd gone wrong.

Part II Advanced

The teacher repeats the stimuli of the second drill of Part I and the students respond as in the example.

Example
TEACHER: I explained. Then he understood.
STUDENT: It wasn't until I'd explained that he understood.

To simplify this, the teacher may use the stimulus:
He didn't understand until I'd explained.

UNIT **81** *Intermediate and Advanced*

To practise the PAST PERFECT SIMPLE *with* no sooner.

Part I

Example
TEACHER: I took off my raincoat, and immediately it began to rain again.
STUDENT: I'd no sooner taken off my raincoat than it began to rain again.

●*Drill*
He got into bed, and immediately he fell asleep.
We sat down, and immediately the telephone rang.
He bought a car, and immediately he had an accident.
They reached the beach, and immediately it started to rain.
The concert finished, and immediately the audience began clapping.
The aeroplane took off, and immediately one of the engines failed.
He got on the train, and immediately it left.
She took off her coat, and immediately she began to feel cold.
I opened the window, and immediately she said there was a draught.
The students finished the exercise, and immediately the teacher gave them another.
He arrived at the party, and immediately he got a phone call to return home.
She married him, and immediately she regretted it.
I put my knife and fork down, and immediately the waiter took my plate.

He put up his umbrella, and immediately it stopped raining.
He lit a cigarette, and immediately he began to cough.
I said it, and immediately I realised I was wrong.
He read the letter, and immediately he tore it up.
The band started to play, and immediately they started to dance.
I sharpened the pencil, and immediately it broke again.
She came into the room, and immediately she complained of the heat.
He began to speak, and immediately she interrupted him.
She lent me the book, and immediately she asked for it back.
She shut the door, and immediately she remembered that she'd forgotten her keys.
She read the letter, and immediately she burst into tears.
He took the job, and immediately he fell ill.
We washed up the breakfast things, and immediately we started to prepare the lunch.
He settled in (Cambridge), and immediately he had to move to (London).
I said it, and immediately I wished I hadn't.
He recovered from one cold, and immediately he caught another.
He stood up, and immediately he was told to sit down again.

Part II

The teacher repeats the stimuli of the drill above and the students respond as in the example.

Example

TEACHER: I took off my raincoat, and immediately it began to rain again.
STUDENT: No sooner had I taken off my raincoat than it began to rain again.

Alternatively, the teacher may use the stimulus:
'I'd no sooner taken off my raincoat than it began to rain again.'

THE PAST PERFECT CONTINUOUS

To introduce the PAST PERFECT CONTINUOUS *by means of actions.*

Method   The teacher first writes these time lengths on the blackboard:

FOR A SHORT TIME
FOR A LITTLE WHILE
FOR A FEW SECONDS

He then performs the actions that follow in pairs, commenting on each pair, as indicated. He then repeats each pair of actions and, indicating the time phrase to be used, requires the students to give the comments, beginning: 'After you'd been . . .'

● *Drill*

The teacher looks out of the window. He sits down.	After I'd been looking out of the window for a short time, I sat down.
He sits down. He starts to write.	After I'd been sitting down for a little while, I started to write.
He writes. He begins to read.	After I'd been writing for a few seconds, I began to read.
He reads. He closes the book.	After I'd been reading for a short time, I closed the book.
He writes. He puts away his pen.	After I'd been writing for a few seconds, I put away my pen.
He sits down. He stands up.	After I'd been sitting down for a short time, I stood up.
He sits down. He goes to sleep.	After I'd been sitting down for a little while, I went to sleep.
He reads. He looks at his watch.	After I'd been reading for a short time, I looked at my watch.
He reads. He turns over the page.	After I'd been reading for a few seconds, I turned over the page.
He walks around. He opens the window.	After I'd been walking around for a little while, I opened the window.

He writes. He moves the table.	After I'd been writing for a little while, I moved the table.
He draws on the blackboard. He rubs the drawings off.	After I'd been drawing for a few seconds, I rubbed my drawings off.
He looks at a magazine. He gives it to a student.	After I'd been looking at the magazine for a short time, I gave it to Mr X.
He sleeps. He wakes up suddenly.	After I'd been sleeping for a little while, I woke up suddenly.
He lights a match and lets it burn. He blows it out.	After the match had been burning for a few seconds, I blew it out.

UNIT **83**   *Intermediate*

To practise after + *the* PAST PERFECT CONTINUOUS, *used with the* SIMPLE PAST.

Example
TEACHER: They drove for three hours. Then they stopped for lunch.
STUDENT: After they'd been driving for three hours, they stopped for lunch.

●*Drill*
She saved her money for six months. Then she went on holiday.
We decorated the room for three hours. Then we stopped for tea.
I mowed the lawn for half an hour. Then I went in for lunch.
She did her homework for an hour. Then she watched the television.
The pilot flew around for three hours. Then he landed the plane in a field.
We walked for an hour. Then we sat down for a rest.
He learnt English for a year. Then he took the exam.
She studied French for six months. Then she went to France.
He took her out for six months. Then he got engaged to her.
He lectured for half an hour. Then he had a drink of water.
We played records for an hour and a half. Then we went out for a drink.
He waited for her for an hour. Then he went home.
I sat in the chair for ten minutes. Then I went off to sleep.
She lived in (London) for ten years. Then she moved to (Bristol).
They danced for half an hour. Then he bought her some refreshments.
He worked there for five years. Then he found another job.
I smoked my pipe for ten minutes. Then it went out.
They watched television for two hours. Then they turned it off.
He looked at her for five minutes. Then she smiled at him.
The secretary typed letters for two hours. Then she left the office.

UNIT 84   *Intermediate*

To practise the PAST PERFECT CONTINUOUS *with* only,

used with when *and the* SIMPLE PAST.

Method   The students are required to join the two ideas presented by the teacher as in the example, adding an appropriate time phrase with *for*. Before beginning the drill, the teacher should point out that the use of *only* here implies *less time than expected,* and he should make sure that the students choose a time phrase that does not conflict with this meaning and that they produce suitable stress and intonation.

Example
TEACHER: He was staying at the hotel. He decided to leave.
STUDENT: He'd only been staying at the hotel for two days when he
           decided to leave.

●*Drill*
She was studying her lesson. Her sister interrupted her.
I was walking. I got tired and stopped.
He was writing. His pen ran out of ink.
She was sitting in the chair. She dropped off to sleep.
He was wearing the suit. He tore the jacket.
We were doing our exercises. Our friends arrived.
She was learning English. She took her first exam.
I was mowing the lawn. It began to rain.
She was sleeping. We woke her up.
The fire was burning. The firemen put it out.
He was learning to drive. He had an accident.
She was sitting down. She stood up again.
He was running. He got cramp.
He was working there. He got the sack.
They were living in London. They decided to move.
We were driving. The car broke down.
He was going out with her. He asked her to marry him.
She was watching the television. She switched it off.
I was waiting for the bus. It came.
She was learning French. She gave it up.

UNIT 85 *Intermediate*

To practise the PAST PERFECT CONTINUOUS *followed by*
before *with the* SIMPLE PAST.

Note Before beginning the drill, the teacher should point out that, in their contexts, the periods of time given below all imply *longer than expected*. He should make sure that the students produce the correct stress and intonation to convey this meaning.

Method The students combine the teacher's two statements, as in the example.

Example
TEACHER: He looked at the photo for ten minutes. Then he realised it was the wrong one.
STUDENT: He'd been looking at the photo for ten minutes before he realised it was the wrong one.

● *Drill*
She learnt English for ten years. Then she came/went to England.
They travelled for six hours. Then they stopped for a meal.
He wrote letters for an hour and a half. Then he ran out of envelopes.
I drove for five hours. Then I started to feel tired.
He broke into houses for nine months. Then the police caught him.
They walked for four hours. Then they had a rest.
He gambled for three years. Then his wife found out.
She tried on hats for an hour. Then she bought one.
We lay in the sun for three hours. Then we moved into the shade.
She took ten photos. Then she realised there was no film in the camera.
I looked for it for days. Then I found it.
He worked on the problem for a week. Then he solved it.
We waited for the bus for twenty-five minutes. Then it came.
I sat at the table for a quarter of an hour. Then the waiter took my order.
He listened to the music for half an hour. Then he recognised the composer.
She called him for five minutes. Then he answered.
They knocked on the door for ten minutes. Then she let them in.
He wore those old trousers for three years. Then he had them cleaned.
The teacher explained it for half an hour. Then they understood.
I expected the letter for three months. Then it arrived.

UNIT **86**   *Advanced*

To practise the special use of the PAST PERFECT

CONTINUOUS.

Note The Past Perfect Continuous is sometimes used for a previous action whose result is still continuing (at a stated time in the past) although the action itself has ceased. This use of the Past Perfect Continuous is equivalent (in past time) to the use of the Present Perfect Continuous described and practised in Unit 63 (see Note, p. 93).
  cf. He's got a black eye (this evening) because he'*s been fighting.*
      He'd got a . black eye (yesterday afternoon) because he'*d been fighting.*

Method The teacher asks the following questions, which the students answer, using the cues provided, with the verb in the Past Perfect Continuous.

Example
TEACHER: Why were they brown?   sunbathe
STUDENT: They were brown because they'd been sunbathing.

●*Drill*

Why had she got flour on her hands?	make a cake
Why was he miserable?	take an exam
Why did he look half asleep?	rest
Why was she crying?	peel onions
Why were you out of breath?	run
Why did they feel exhausted?	travel all day
Why was he carrying a camera?	take photos
Why had he got oil on his hands?	mend the car
Why had you got indigestion?	eat too fast
Why were his trousers torn?	climb trees
Why were you sweating?	lie in the sun
Why was he wearing overalls?	clean the garage
Why was he soaking wet?	stand in the rain
Why had he lost a lot of money?	bet on horses
Why were his hands dirty?	garden
Why was he wearing shorts?	play tennis
Why had he got a nasty taste in his mouth?	eat raw onions
Why did your feet ache?	wear tight shoes
Why was he carrying a hammer and nails?	mend the fence
Why was the grass wet?	rain

The drill may then be repeated to get shorter answers from the students.

Example
TEACHER: Why were they brown?
STUDENT: Because they'd been sunbathing.

THE PRESENT CONTINUOUS FOR FUTURE

To introduce the PRESENT CONTINUOUS *for a* PLANNED

or ARRANGED FUTURE.

Method Before beginning the drill, the teacher points out that for the first group of questions *Where* will be used, for the second, *What,* and for the third, *When.* He then conducts the drill according to the following example.

Example
TEACHER: Where are you going tomorrow?
STUDENT: I'm going to (London).

●*Drill*
Where are you meeting your friend?
Where are you going for your holidays?
Where are you having lunch today?
Where are you taking your friends tonight?
Where are you going after school?
Where are you having the party?
Where are you spending the weekend?
Where are you putting your new chair?
Where are you playing (tennis)?
Where are you leaving the car tonight?

What are you doing on Sunday morning?
What are you doing this evening?
What are you doing tomorrow afternoon?
What are you doing this weekend?
What are you doing during the (Easter) holidays?
What are you giving him for his birthday?
What are you having for lunch today?
What are you taking with you for the weekend?
What are you wearing to the party?
What are you cooking for dinner tonight?

When are you having your next lesson?
When are you having them to dinner?
When are you having lunch today?
When are you having a bath?
When are you having another driving lesson?

When are you meeting your friend?
When are you coming to school again?
When are you taking the exam?
When are you going to the theatre?
When are you taking your holiday this year?
When are you going shopping?
When are you seeing her again?

UNIT 88   *Intermediate*

To practise the PRESENT CONTINUOUS *for a* PLANNED *or*

ARRANGED FUTURE.

Example
TEACHER: I've decided to leave at four o'clock.
STUDENT: I'm leaving at four o'clock.

●*Drill*
I've decided to get up early tomorrow.
I've decided to go to bed early this evening.
I've decided to stay in this evening.
I've decided to buy her a watch for her birthday.
I've decided to catch the 12.28 to (London).
I've decided to have lunch on the train.
I've decided to close the shop early tonight.
I've decided to have a party this evening.
I've decided to give him a fountain-pen for Christmas.
I've decided to go out for a walk later on.
I've decided to have my hair cut this afternoon.
I've decided to eat out on Saturday evening.

Example
TEACHER: He's arranged to telephone me tonight.
STUDENT: He's telephoning me tonight.

●*Drill*
We've arranged to have a party next Friday.
I've arranged to spend a few days in (Cambridge) next week.
Peter's arranged to call for me at eight o'clock.
She's arranged to take her exam in December.
I've arranged to see the doctor tomorrow.
My friend's arranged to come to stay with me next weekend.
We've arranged to have lunch at one o'clock.
I've arranged to take her out on Saturday.
They've arranged to go to (Spain) for their holidays this year.

Mary's arranged to play tennis at three o'clock tomorrow afternoon.
Mr Brown's arranged to have his house painted next month.
We've arranged to have the sitting room decorated soon.
I've arranged to borrow his car at the weekend.
I've arranged to have my eyes tested next Wednesday.
They've arranged to have the car serviced next week.
Mr Smith's arranged to catch the 12.32 to (Birmingham).
He's arranged to stay in (Birmingham) for three days.
He's arranged to come back on Friday.
His wife's arranged to meet him at the station in the car.

UNIT **89**   *Intermediate*

To practise the PRESENT CONTINUOUS *for a* PLANNED *or*

ARRANGED FUTURE.

Method   The teacher asks the questions, requiring the students to reply
with 'No', and the Present Continuous with an appropriate future time
phrase.

Example
TEACHER: Has she left school yet?
STUDENT: No. She's leaving at the end of the term.

●*Drill*
Have they had their party yet?
Has he taken her out yet?
Have you had your photo taken yet?
Has he visited his uncle in hospital yet?
Has your friend made his speech yet?
Have you driven his new car yet?
Has the electrician come yet?
Have they had lunch yet?
Have you bought her birthday present yet?
Has he telephoned yet?
Have they moved into their new house yet?
Has she begun her new job yet?
Has he had the house painted yet?
Has she started school yet?
Has he paid you back yet?
Has she come out of hospital yet?
Have you worn your new suit/dress yet?
Has she booked seats yet?
Has he got back yet?
Have you taken your exam yet?

UNIT 90   *Intermediate*

To practise the PRESENT CONTINUOUS *for a* PLANNED *or*

ARRANGED FUTURE.

Method The teacher asks the following questions about an Arranged Future. The students answer with *because* and a second Arranged Future, using the cues provided, as in the example.

Example
TEACHER: Why are you going to (London) on Saturday? visit my uncle
STUDENT: I'm going to (London) on Saturday because I'm visiting my uncle.

● *Drill*

Why are you having breakfast early tomorrow?	go to (London)
Why are you selling your old car?	buy a new one
Why are you visiting your cousin tomorrow afternoon?	leave for America
Why are you staying at home tomorrow?	have some friends in
Why are you leaving school early today?	meet my mother
Why are you having your hair cut on Friday?	go to a dance
Why are you staying away from class tomorrow?	take an exam
Why are you going to bed early tonight?	get up early
Why is he going to the tailor's tomorrow?	have a fitting for a new suit
Why is she buying a new dress tomorrow?	go to a party
Why are you going to the dentist tomorrow?	have a tooth filled
Why are the children going to the zoo on Sunday?	go back to school on Monday
Why is he going out with the boys on Friday?	get married on Saturday
Why are they cancelling their holiday?	buy a car instead
Why are you buying a new violin?	give a recital
Why is she giving a party?	go abroad next Thursday
Why is he hiring a car at the weekend?	take his wife out
Why are you buying a new suite?	get rid of the old one
Why are they selling their stair carpet?	move to a bungalow
Why is he getting a new piano?	take up music again
Why is she changing her flat?	start a new job
Why is he giving up his job?	emigrate to Australia
Why is he going on a diet?	play football next winter
Why are they meeting at the station?	travel to (Brighton)
Why is Professor Black getting a present?	retire

UNIT 91   *Intermediate*

To practise the PRESENT CONTINUOUS *negative for a* REFUSAL.

Notes 1. The Present Continuous may be used to express Refusal. With the 1st Person, it expresses a straightforward refusal on the part of the speaker (e.g. 'I'm not waiting any longer' = 'I refuse to wait any longer!'). With the 2nd and 3rd Persons, it expresses the speaker's refusal to allow an action (e.g. 'He's not bringing that in here' = 'I refuse to allow him to bring that in here').

    2. The first drill of this unit practises the use with the 1st Person; the second drill practises the use with the 2nd and 3rd Persons. In both drills the word *not* should be stressed—the stronger the stress the more emphatic the refusal. In the second drill the contracted forms *'re not, 's not* should be used rather than the forms *aren't, isn't*; although with proper stress and intonation the latter would also be correct, the former are more emphatic and therefore probably more commonly used for refusals.

    3. It is not desirable to practise this pattern until *won't* for Refusal has been mastered, nor is it necessary to practise both drills at the same time. In fact, the teacher may think it sufficient to limit practice of this use to the 1st Person only. This unit may be used in conjunction with Unit 97, p. 133 (*not going to* used for a Refusal).

Example
TEACHER: I refuse to sit on that hard seat.
STUDENT: I'm not sitting on that hard seat.

●*Drill*
I refuse to lend you my pen again.
I refuse to wait any longer.
I refuse to do that again.
I refuse to walk any farther.
I refuse to go out in this rain.
I refuse to come here again.
I refuse to give him a penny.
I refuse to stay up later than midnight.
I refuse to pay in advance.
I refuse to take orders from anyone.
I refuse to drink vodka again.
I refuse to answer the telephone any more.
I refuse to have anything to do with her.
I refuse to listen to any more nonsense.
I refuse to work late any more this week.
I refuse to tolerate rudeness.
I refuse to sit through that film again.
I refuse to help you any more.

I refuse to give any opinion.
I refuse to give my consent to the proposal.
I refuse to wear that horrible tie/scarf.
I refuse to lend him money again.
I refuse to eat in that restaurant again.
I refuse to discuss my affairs with him.
I refuse to spend £5 on a meal.
I refuse to accept any excuses.
I refuse to put any money in that business.
I refuse to have that sort of person here.
I refuse to agree to that.
I refuse to hang about here any longer.

Example
TEACHER: I won't allow you to leave that there.
STUDENT: You're not leaving that there.

●*Drill*
I won't allow you to drive my car again.
I won't allow him to treat me like that.
I won't allow you to use my fountain-pen again.
I won't allow you to invite him here.
I won't allow you to gamble in my house.
I won't allow him to come here drunk.
I won't allow him to borrow any more of my records.
I won't allow her to use my sitting room for her committee meetings.
I won't allow you to bring that good-for-nothing to my party.
I won't allow them to have political meetings in my house.
I won't allow you to use my best scissors to cut paper.
I won't allow her to lie in bed all day tomorrow.
I won't allow her to make any more long-distance calls from this phone.
I won't allow you to stay out late until after the exam.
I won't allow you to read any more of those comics.

THE 'GOING TO' FUTURE

To introduce going to *for* INTENTION *in the Future by means of actions.*

Method The teacher does the actions in the first group below, commenting as instructed. He then repeats the actions, asking as he prepares to do each one: 'What am I going to do?' The students reply: 'You're going to . . .' and the teacher then does the action. When the first group has been completed in this way, the teacher repeats the procedure with the second group.

●*Drill*

The teacher picks up a piece of chalk, goes to the blackboard, holds the chalk up to write, says: 'I'm going to write on the blackboard,' and then writes something.

The teacher pulls out his chair, stands in front of it says: 'I'm going to sit down', and then sits down.

The teacher goes to the light switch, puts his hand on it, says: 'I'm going to switch on the light', and then switches it on.

The teacher goes to the door, puts his hand on the door-handle, says: 'I'm going to open the door', and then opens it.

The teacher takes his comb out of his pocket, says: 'I'm going to comb my hair', and then combs it.

The teacher takes a box of matches out of his pocket, takes out a match, says: 'I'm going to strike a match', and then strikes it.

The teacher takes his handkerchief out of his pocket, says: 'I'm going to blow my nose', and then blows it.

The teacher picks up the duster, goes to the blackboard, holds the duster up to wipe the board, says: 'I'm going to wipe the blackboard', and then wipes it.

The teacher picks up a book, walks over to a student, says: 'I'm going to give this book to Mr X', and then gives it to him.

The teacher tears up a piece of paper, walks over to the waste-paper basket, says: 'I'm going to throw this paper into the waste-paper basket', and throws it in.

UNIT 93	*Elementary and Intermediate*

To practise going to *for* INTENTION *in the Future.*

Part I Elementary

Example

TEACHER TO STUDENT A:	Ask B if he's going to write the letter in pencil or in ink.
STUDENT A TO STUDENT B:	Are you going to write the letter in pencil or in ink?
STUDENT B TO STUDENT A:	I'm going to write the letter in ink.
*TEACHER TO STUDENT A:	What does he say?
STUDENT A:	He says he's going to write the letter in ink.

*It should be possible for the teacher to leave out 'What does he say?' once the students have grasped the form of the drill.

●*Drill*

Are you going to change before or after tea?
Are you going to play jazz or dance music this evening?
Are you going to buy her perfume or lipstick?
Are you going to travel to (London) by car or by train?
Are you going to have lunch at home or in a restaurant?
Are you going to make coffee or tea?
Are you going to put it in the sitting room or in the dining room?
Are you going to wear a suit or a sweater tonight?
Are you going to send a postcard or a letter?
Are you going to invite Susan or Diana to the dance?
Are you going to finish work early or late tonight?
Are you going to take the exam this year or next year?
Are you going to read the newspaper or your book?
Are you going to mend the lamp before or after dinner?
Are you going to sit near the window or near the door?
Are you going to listen to the radio or watch television?
Are you going to telephone or send a letter?
Are you going to catch a bus or walk?
Are you going to camp or stay in a hotel?
Are you going to write the letter or type it?

Part II Intermediate

Example

TEACHER TO STUDENT A:	Ask B what time he's going to meet his friends this evening.
STUDENT A TO STUDENT B:	What time are you going to meet your friends this evening?
STUDENT B TO STUDENT A:	I'm going to meet my friends at seven o'clock.
*TEACHER TO STUDENT A:	What does he say?
STUDENT A:	He says he's going to meet his friends at seven o'clock.

*It should be possible for the teacher to leave out 'What does he say?' once the students have grasped the form of the drill.

● *Drill*

What time are you going to put on the television?
What time are you going to have breakfast tomorrow?
What time are you going to leave the house this evening?
What time are you going to start your homework?
What time are you going to get up on Sunday?

Where are you going to take her this evening?
Where are you going to hide the money?
Where are you going to sit next lesson?
Where are you going to leave the message?
Where are you going to hang that picture?

What are you going to wear to the party?
What are you going to buy with the money?
What are you going to cook for lunch?
What are you going to take away with you?
What are you going to have for dinner?

When are you going to do your homework?
When are you going to telephone him?
When are you going to write to your parents?
When are you going to visit them again?
When are you going to cash the cheque?
When are you going to send him a telegram?
When are you going to begin your exercises?
When are you going to pay back the money?
When are you going to come and see us?
When are you going to show me the photos?

How long are you going to stay here?
How many examples are you going to write?
How much money are you going to lend him?
How are you going to travel to (America)?
How many bottles of wine are you going to buy?
How long are you going to spend in the coffee bar?
How many tickets are you going to get?
How long are you going to watch television this evening?

How many books are you going to borrow from the library?
How long are you going to study at this school?
What are you going to do after lunch?
What are you going to do this evening?
What are you going to do on Sunday?
What are you going to do after school?
What are you going to do in (London)?
What are you going to do next year?
What are you going to do tomorrow afternoon?
What are you going to do at the weekend?
What are you going to do next Wednesday?
What are you going to do after tea?

UNIT **94**   *Intermediate*

To practise going to *for* INTENTION *in the Future.*

Example
TEACHER: They intend to play records this evening.
STUDENT: They're going to play records this evening.

●*Drill*
I intend to buy a new car.
He intends to take his girl-friend out on Saturday.
They intend to sell their house soon.
She intends to have a bath.
He intends to get tickets this afternoon.
I intend to close the shop early this evening.
We intend to decorate the front room soon.
They intend to dig up this part of the road next week.
I intend to get another job.
He intends to grow a beard.
We intend to work harder next term.
I intend to stop for petrol in a minute.
He intends to telephone his friend this afternoon.
I intend to ask her for her opinion.
That little boy intends to be an engine-driver.
She intends to learn to type.
I intend to light the fire.
She intends to make a cup of tea at four o'clock.
He intends to leave school at the end of the term.
John intends to start learning Russian soon.

Do you intend to eat all that?
Do they intend to book seats?
Do you intend to finish that tonight?
Does she intend to make the beds?
Do you intend to buy me another drink?
Does he intend to get his hair cut?
Does he intend to buy her a birthday present?
Do you intend to wear your new suit to the party?
Does he intend to work late tonight?

He doesn't intend to take her out tomorrow.
I don't intend to have any lunch today.
They don't intend to grow tulips this year.
She doesn't intend to come until four o'clock.
They don't intend to take the exam.
We don't intend to change our car till next year.
I don't intend to go to the football match this week.
He doesn't intend to cash the cheque till Saturday.
Mother doesn't intend to cook the lunch tomorrow.
She doesn't intend to sell her house after all.

UNIT **95**   *Intermediate*

To practise going to *used to express the* SPEAKER'S

CERTAINTY *about the Future.*

Example
TEACHER: I feel sure it'll be very difficult.
STUDENT: It's going to be very difficult.

●*Drill*
I feel sure it'll be cold tomorrow.
I feel sure that car will crash in a minute.
I feel sure you'll miss the train.
I feel sure I shall be sick.
I feel sure it'll rain soon.
I feel sure that cyclist will fall off his bicycle soon.
I feel sure it'll be very painful.
I feel sure we shall make a lot of money out of this.
I feel sure he'll be very happy about the news.
I feel sure we shall be late.
I feel sure the bridge will collapse.
I feel sure this holiday will be expensive.
I feel sure she'll be very hungry.
I feel sure their party will be terrible.
I feel sure he'll fail his exam.

Example

TEACHER: I feel sure he won't win the game.
STUDENT: He isn't/He's not going to win the game.

(*Note* The contracted forms *isn't/aren't* are more usual, but *'s not*, *'re not* may be used, particularly if special emphasis is required.)

●*Drill*

I feel sure he won't get there in time.
I feel sure they won't be very pleased about it.
I feel sure she won't pass her driving test.
I feel sure they won't change the arrangements because of her.
I feel sure it won't be a heavy storm.
I feel sure they won't finish in time.
I feel sure it won't last very long.
I feel sure we shan't make a profit on that.

UNIT 96   *Intermediate*

To practise going to *used to express the* SPEAKER'S

CERTAINTY *about the Future.*

Method The teacher provides the stimulus. The students repeat this and add a second statement using *going to* and the cue provided.

Example

TEACHER: The clouds are lifting.   stop raining
STUDENT: The clouds are lifting. It's going
                to stop raining.

●*Drill*

I must leave the room.	be sick
He isn't working hard enough.	fail the exam
That car's going too fast.	crash
I've forgotten to post his letter.	he/be angry
He thinks he'll pass the exam.	be disappointed
The clouds are going away.	it/clear up soon
That aeroplane's coming down.	land
We've missed the bus.	arrive late
Look at that dog in the middle of the road.	get run over
He doesn't know the truth yet.	get a shock
She's driving very carelessly.	hit that tree
Turn off the milk.	boil over
They're very late.	miss the beginning
Her dress is too tight.	split
Hurry up!	be late
Look at those clouds!	it/pour with rain

The weather's very cold today. I think . . .	freeze
He's a difficult person. I think . . .	have trouble with him
This bridge feels rather unsafe. I think . . .	collapse soon
I feel dizzy. I think . . .	faint
That ship's in trouble. I think . . .	sink
The sky looks very grey. I think . . .	snow
Our horse has moved out in front. I think . . .	win
You shouldn't have hit him so hard. I think . . .	have a black eye
The cat's eating a lot these days. I think . . .	have kittens
Don't rely on the rope. I think . . .	break

UNIT **97**   *Intermediate*

To practise not going to *for a* REFUSAL.

Notes   1. *not going to* (like the Present Continuous, negative) is used to express Refusal. With the 1st Person, it expresses a straightforward refusal on the part of the speaker (e.g. 'I'm not going to wait any longer.' = 'I refuse to wait any longer.') With the 2nd and 3rd Persons, it expresses the speaker's refusal to allow an action (e.g. 'He's not going to bring that in here.' = 'I refuse to allow him to bring that in here.')

2. The first part of the following drill practises the use of the 1st Person, the second part practises the use with the 2nd and 3rd Persons. For note on the use of stress and contracted forms see Unit 91, Note 2.

3. It is not desirable to practise this pattern until *won't* for Refusal has been mastered, nor is it necessary to practise both parts of the drill at the same time. In fact, the teacher may think it sufficient to limit practice of this idea to the 1st Person only. This drill may be used in conjunction with Drill 91, p. 125.

Example
TEACHER: I refuse to answer any more questions.
STUDENT: I'm not going to answer any more questions.

●*Drill*
I refuse to stay here another second.
I refuse to sleep in that bed.
I refuse to tidy up after them.
I refuse to eat any more of that.
I refuse to lend you my car again.
I refuse to have that student in my class.
I refuse to walk all that way.
I refuse to remind her about it again.

I refuse to talk about it any more.
I refuse to play cards with you again.
I refuse to pay (£5) for a ticket.
I refuse to argue about it.
I refuse to explain it again.
I refuse to take orders from him.
I refuse to carry it all that way.
I refuse to invite them again.
I refuse to tell you again.
I refuse to put up with that sort of behaviour.
I refuse to sit and watch television all the evening.
I refuse to do it again.
I refuse to accept work like that.
I refuse to waste time doing that.
I refuse to wait in all day for them.
I refuse to drive with him again.
I refuse to turn out on a night like this.

Example
TEACHER: I won't let him cheat me again.
STUDENT: He's not going to cheat me again.

●*Drill*
I won't allow him to come here again.
I won't allow him to see you again.
I won't let him treat me like a child.
I won't let you borrow my bicycle again.
I won't allow you to lift that by yourself.
I won't allow her to get away with it this time.
I won't let him catch me out again.
I won't allow them to make a fool of me.
I won't allow him to tell me what to do.
I won't let you come out with me looking like that.
I won't allow them to play football in my garden.
I won't allow you to come in here with those muddy shoes on.
I won't let you use my hair-drier again.
I won't allow them to have it all their own way.
I won't allow her to talk me into it.

SHALL AND WILL

To practise shall *and* will ('ll) *to express the* PURE

FUTURE.

Note   *Shall* and *will* are used to express the Pure Future: when the future state, condition or action is not controlled by human will but is the result of external circumstances.

It has been stated elsewhere (see Unit 12, p. 16, Note) that Verbs of Perception and Non-Conclusive Verbs normally express states or conditions that are beyond our control; therefore, the future of such verbs is usually expressed by *shall* and *will*. This drill practises these verbs in the future. A few other verbs are included, but only in cases where they refer to situations that are dependent on external circumstances, e.g. 'We *shan't go* to bed till midnight' implies: 'We *can't* go before this (because there is something preventing us and we can't help it).' Compare: 'We *aren't going* to bed . . .' which implies: 'We don't intend to go . . .'

Method   The teacher gives a sentence in the past and the students express the same idea in the future, using *shall* or *will*. The contracted forms ('*ll, shan't, won't*) should be used whenever possible.

    Example
TEACHER: She forgave him.
STUDENT: She'll forgive him.

  ●*Drill*
I knew the result at ten o'clock.
He believed the story.
She understood eventually.
I had time to help after lunch.
He recognised her at once.
He remembered that day for a long time.
She saw your note.
He felt better later on.
She forgot to bring them.
He realised his mistake.
He found out in the end.
Tuesday was the . . . day of . . .
She noticed the difference.

I heard the bell.
He had to do it quickly.
Her birthday fell on a Saturday.
I thought of it later.
He was twenty-one on Christmas Eve.
She found something wrong with it.
It meant going out in the rain.
He needed some more money.
It cost £25.
The baby was born in April.
The cut healed quickly.
It looked silly.
It tasted too sweet.
The committee consisted of six members.
The job required patience.
He refused to do it.
The dress suited her well.

Did he understand it?
Did she mind waiting?
Did she discover the truth?
When did you know for certain?
Did it matter?
Did she remember?
How long did the journey take?
Did they enjoy it?
What time did it finish?
Did he do it properly?
Did he agree?
When was it ready?
Did it look all right?
Did it appear rude?
Were the shops open in the afternoon?
What did it taste like?
How did it fit him?
Did he get the answer right?
Did it get cooler in the evening?
When did it get dark?
Did she like it?
Did his hair grow again?
How much did you need?
Did the regulations apply to everyone?
How long did the film last?

He wasn't ready in time.
It didn't cost much.
We didn't have enough money.
That didn't matter.
I didn't have to wait.
He didn't mind.
The colour didn't fade.

He didn't know the answer for three weeks.
The sun didn't set until six o'clock.
He didn't need an overcoat.
She didn't have time to do it.
I didn't feel disappointed.
She didn't believe him.
We didn't go to bed till midnight.
The carpet didn't go with the curtains.
Her father didn't object to the marriage.
That didn't sound very nice.
The lesson didn't finish till four o'clock.
Her gloves didn't match her handbag.
He didn't trust her after that.

UNIT **99** *Intermediate*

To contrast going to (*Intention*) *and* shall/will (*Pure Future*) *with* if.

Method First the students answer the teacher's question, supplying a suitable adverb of future time. Then they change the sentence, using the Future Tense and the *if*-clause supplied by the teacher. The contracted form *'ll* should be used throughout the drill.

Example
TEACHER: When are you going to write to her?
STUDENT: I'm going to write to her this afternoon.
TEACHER: if I've got time
STUDENT: I'll write to her this afternoon if I've got time.

● *Drill*

When are you going to play tennis?	if it doesn't rain
When is he going to buy a new car?	if he's saved up enough money
When is she going to telephone him?	if she doesn't get a letter
When is he going to leave college?	if he passes the exam
When are you going to have a bath?	if the water's hot enough
When are you going to get your hair cut?	if the shop/hairdresser's isn't too crowded
When is he going to wear that new tie?	if his wife lets him
When are they going to sell their house?	if they can get a good price
When is she going to take the exam?	if she's ready for it
When are you going to open that bottle?	if Peter comes round
When are you going to do it?	if you like
When are you going to call in to see me?	if that's convenient
When is he going to see the doctor?	if he doesn't feel better

When is she going to finish the work? if nothing goes wrong
When are you going to tidy up the garden? if it's fine
When is he going to pay them back? if his money comes through
When is she going to put up the curtains? if they're dry
When are you going to post the letter? if I can find a stamp

UNIT **100**   *Intermediate*

To practise shall *and* will (*Pure Future*) *with* if.

Method The teacher asks questions in the pattern: 'What will you do if . . .?' The students supply their own answers, using the contracted form *'ll* throughout the drill.

Example
TEACHER: What will you do if you can't get a yellow one?
STUDENT: If I can't get a yellow one, I'll buy a red one.

●*Drill*
What will you do if it rains?
What will you do if you don't like the record?
What will you do if you miss the bus?
What will you do if you don't pass your exam?
What will you do if you are free tomorrow?
What will you do if the weather gets cold?
What will you do if your money doesn't arrive?
What will you do if the cinema's full?
What will you do if nobody can come to the party?
What will you do if you run out of petrol?
What will you do if the train's late?
What will you do if you can't get a cheap one?
What will you do if you win the money?
What will you do if you lose your way?
What will you do if you don't get a letter?
What will you do if you fail the test?
What will you do if he doesn't phone?
What will you do if the price goes up?
What will you do if she forgets to come?
What will you do if your watch stops again?
What will you do if you can't find it in the dictionary?
What will you do if it finishes early?
What will you do if the shop is closed?
What will you do if the weather gets any colder?
What will you do if you can't come next Friday?

UNIT **101**   *Intermediate*

To practise Will you . . .? *for a* REQUEST.

Example

TEACHER: I want/I'd like you to close the door.
STUDENT: Will you close the door, please?

● *Drill*
I want you to open the window.
I'd like you to wait a minute.
I want you to buy me some stamps.
I'd like you to post these letters.
I want you to lend me that record.
I'd like you to carry these things downstairs.
I want you to keep quiet.
I'd like you to buy me some cigarettes.
I want you to telephone me this evening.
I'd like you to help me with the washing-up.
I want you to do something for me.
I'd like you to ring for a taxi.
I want you to make your bed.
I'd like you to sign this letter.
I want you to give him a message.
I'd like you to lay the table.
I want you to show me your passport.
I'd like you to wake me up at six o'clock.
I want you to listen carefully.
I'd like you to bring a bottle with you.

Example

TEACHER TO STUDENT A: Ask B to explain it again.
STUDENT A TO STUDENT B: Will you explain it again, please?

● *Drill*
Ask B to give you a light.
Ask B to tell you the answer.
Ask B to buy you a newspaper.
Ask B to carry your bag.
Ask B to pass the ashtray.
Ask B to speak more clearly.
Ask B to fetch you a plate.

Ask B to help you on with your coat.
Ask B to lend you his dictionary.
Ask B to excuse you.
Ask B to clear the table.
Ask B to turn off the radio.
Ask B to get the tickets.
Ask B to look after your case.
Ask B to lock the back door.

The above drills may then be repeated, with *will* used in a Question Tag.

Example
TEACHER: I want you to close the door.
STUDENT: Close the door, will you?

UNIT **102**   *Intermediate*

To practise Shall I . . .? *for an* OFFER.

Example
TEACHER: Do you want/Would you like me to close the window?
STUDENT: Shall I close the window?

●*Drill*
Do you want me to fetch your coat?
Would you like me to get you some matches?
Do you want me to carry your bag?
Would you like me to help you on with your coat?
Do you want me to drive you home?
Would you like me to give you the answer?
Do you want me to put it over there?
Would you like me to do it for you?
Do you want me to lend you some money?
Would you like me to give you a lift?
Do you want me to put some sugar in your coffee?
Would you like me to start now?
Do you want me to switch the fire on?
Would you like me to wear this tie?
Do you want me to play you my new record?

Example

TEACHER: Offer to cut some more sandwiches.
STUDENT: Shall I cut some more sandwiches?

●*Drill*

Offer to write it again.
Offer to draw the curtains.
Offer to put the silver away.
Offer to wash up.
Offer to give him another piece.
Offer to cook it a bit longer.
Offer to sweep the floor.
Offer to show her the photographs.
Offer to play her the records.
Offer to ring for a taxi.

Offer to wind the clock.
Offer to lay the table.
Offer to put it in the fridge.
Offer to close the front door.
Offer to put the car away.
Offer to take in the washing.
Offer to switch off the radio.
Offer to pour Mr X a beer.
Offer to call the lift.
Offer to clean Mr Y's shoes.

The above drills may then be repeated with the response *I'll* . . . and *shall I?* used as a Question Tag.

Example

TEACHER: Do you want me to close the window?
STUDENT: I'll close the window, shall I?

UNIT **103**   *Intermediate*

To practise Shall we . . .? *for a* SUGGESTION.

Note In informal conversation the word *that* would commonly be omitted.

Example

TEACHER: I suggest (that) we have a party.
STUDENT: Shall we have a party?

●*Drill*

I suggest (that) we go for a walk.
                have a game of cards.
                change places.
                go for a drive in the country.
                do the experiment again.
                invite them to dinner.

tell him about it.
sell the house.
have an early night tonight.
play them our new record.
go in for the competition.
have our photograph taken.
eat out on Saturday night.
postpone the meeting.
stop now.

Example
TEACHER: Would it be a good idea for us to buy a new one?
STUDENT: Shall we buy a new one?

●*Drill*
Would it be a good idea for us to leave now?
ask them to dinner one night?
wait till later?
watch television this evening?
paint it green?
write to him about it?
take a taxi?
leave it to him?
go for a picnic?
send her some flowers?
ask Mary and John round for coffee?
hire a car for the weekend?
have dinner now?
take him with us?
ring him up about it?

The above drills may then be repeated with the response *Let's* . . . and
shall we? used as a Question Tag.

Example
TEACHER: I suggest (that) we have a party.
STUDENT: Let's have a party, shall we?

UNIT **104**   *Intermediate*

To practise I'll (I will)/I won't *for a* PROMISE.

Example

TEACHER: I promise to speak to him about it.
STUDENT: I'll speak to him about it.

●*Drill*

I promise to work harder next term.
I promise to buy you an ice-cream.
I promise to get home before eleven o'clock.
I promise to do it carefully.
I promise to come in good time.
I promise to pay you back on Saturday.
I promise to give him a bicycle for his birthday.
I promise to take care of it.
I promise to tell you the answer tomorrow.
I promise to look after it.
I promise to ring you up about it tomorrow.
I promise to write and tell you all about it.
I promise to bring it back on Monday.
I promise to have my hair cut at the weekend.
I promise to help you with it tomorrow.
I promise to light the fire after dinner.
I promise to tidy up after lunch.
I promise to let you have the exercise tomorrow.
I promise to type it carefully.
I promise to shut the gate.

Example

TEACHER: I promise not to do it again.
STUDENT: I won't do it again.

●*Drill*

I promise not to be late.
I promise not to say it again.
I promise not to make it dirty.
I promise not to spend too much.
I promise not to hurt you.
I promise not to take up too much of your time.
I promise not to lose it.
I promise not to tell anyone about it.
I promise not to give you away.
I promise not to go till you come back.

I promise not to damage it.
I promise not to drive too fast.
I promise not to drop it.
I promise not to make that mistake again.
I promise not to mention it to her.

UNIT **105**   *Intermediate*

To practise won't *for a* REFUSAL.

Note   *Won't* for a *Refusal* can be used with things as well as with persons.
This use is practised in the second drill of this unit.

Example
TEACHER: He refuses to pay for her coffee.
STUDENT: He won't pay for her coffee.

●*Drill*
I refuse to do it.
She refuses to listen to him.
I refuse to answer that question.
That dog refuses to stop barking.
He refuses to tell me.
She refuses to speak to him.
The cat refuses to drink this milk.
I refuse to give it up.
They refuse to sell it.
He refuses to admit it.
The budgerigar refuses to come out of its cage.
She refuses to agree to it.
He refuses to believe it.
She refuses to take any notice.
The teacher refuses to help me.
I refuse to explain it again.
He refuses to keep still for five minutes.
His wife refuses to let him wear that tie.
I refuse to eat that food.
The deer refuse to come near us.

Example

TEACHER: This cork refuses to come out.

STUDENT: This cork won't come out.

●*Drill*

This door refuses to open.

This picture refuses to hang straight.

This button refuses to stay done up.

This stain refuses to come out.

The radio refuses to work.

These scissors refuse to cut properly.

His car refuses to start.

My pen refuses to write.

The light refuses to go out.

His false teeth refuse to stay in place.

My hair refuses to curl.

This mark refuses to come off.

My watch refuses to go.

This cut refuses to heal.

My ring refuses to come off.

UNIT **106**   *Intermediate*

To practise will *to express* WILLINGNESS.

Note Compare the following:

(a) He hasn't any money so *I'm going to lend* him some. (= intention)

(b) A   He's come without any money.

B   Really? Oh well, *I'll lend* him some. (= willingness)

In (a) the speaker has had time to think over the situation and come to a decision; the intention to lend the money is premeditated. But in (b) the decision to lend the money is spontaneous, without any previous intention (i.e. B is willing to lend the money although he had not originally intended to).

Method The teacher gives the stimulus and the students respond with *I'll* . . . and the cue provided. The contracted form (*I'll*) should be used throughout.

Example

TEACHER: I've finished my book.   get you another
STUDENT: I'll get you another.

● *Drill*

I've come out without any money.   lend you some
I can't understand this letter.   translate it
The shops are closed on Tuesdays.   go on Friday
I've forgotten to post this letter.   post it
I'm sorry, the cake's finished.   have a biscuit
Professor Sims is very busy today.   wait till tomorrow
The sun's getting in my eyes.   pull the curtains
I've torn my trousers.   mend them
She's not on the phone.   send a telegram
You've missed your bus.   walk
I'm going to clean out the garage.   help you
The visitors have arrived.   get them a drink
The road's under water.   go the other way
Old Mrs Johnson's in hospital.   send her some flowers
The fire's almost out.   get some wood
The typewriter's broken.   write the letter
I'm feeling terribly hungry.   make some sandwiches
There's no chicken left.   have pork
I've left my glasses upstairs.   fetch them
I feel too tired to do the shopping today. do it for you
The telephone's ringing.   answer it
You'll never get there in time.   take a taxi
I'm going to town.   give you a lift
I'm afraid my lawnmower's out of order.   borrow Phillip's
It's terribly hot in here.   open the window
John can't go with you.   go without him
These flowers are dead.   throw them away
It's getting rather dark in here.   switch on the light
One of your tyres is flat.   pump it up
I can't finish all this work.   finish it for you
The fence has fallen down.   put it up
I'm afraid Mr Jarvis is out.   call back tomorrow
This case is rather heavy.   carry it
There's something wrong with it.   take it back to the shop
You forgot to book seats again.   telephone the theatre

THE FUTURE CONTINUOUS

To introduce the FUTURE CONTINUOUS *describing an*

UNFINISHED ACTION *in the Future, by contrasting it with*

the PRESENT CONTINUOUS *describing an* UNFINISHED

ACTION *in the Real Present.*

Method The teacher says a sentence and gives a cue. The students repeat the teacher's sentence and add one of their own, beginning *At this time tomorrow/This time next month* and continuing with the Future Continuous of the verb already used, followed by the cue.

Example
TEACHER: Now he's sitting next to Susan.   Mary
STUDENT: Now he's sitting next to Susan. At this time tomorrow he'll be sitting next to Mary.

● *Drill*

At the moment she's writing a composition.	a letter
Now she's wearing a blue dress.	a red one
At the moment she's cooking fish.	chicken
Now he's reading a book.	a magazine
At the moment the secretary's typing a report.	a letter
Now we're having a language lesson.	a dictation
Now Mr Smith's playing tennis.	golf
At the moment they're eating fish and chips.	roast beef
Now I'm reading Chapter XIII.	Chapter XIV
At the moment they're sitting in the kitchen.	the dining room
Now he's painting the doors.	the windows
At the moment he's visiting the Royal Palace.	the Mosque
Now we're doing Exercise 46.	47
At the moment she's listening to Beethoven.	Mozart
Now they're drinking tea.	coffee

Example

TEACHER: Now they're decorating the sitting room.   the dining room

STUDENT: Now they're decorating the sitting room. This time next month they'll be decorating the dining room.

●*Drill*

Now she's learning English.	French
Now I'm living in (Brighton).	Manchester
Now we're reading "Macbeth".	"Hamlet"
Now I'm studying in (England).	America
Now he's writing his third novel.	his fourth
Now they're performing in Paris.	New York
Now they're skiing in Switzerland.	Austria
Now he's working in Edinburgh.	Glasgow
Now they're showing the film at the Regent.	the Astoria
Now he's going out with Agnes.	someone else

Before doing the above drill, the teacher may wish to use the examples in Unit 20, p. 33, as in the following example:

TEACHER: At the moment he's drinking a glass of whisky.

STUDENT: At the moment he's drinking a glass of whisky.
At this time tomorrow he'll be drinking a glass of whisky.

UNIT **108**   *Intermediate*

To practise the FUTURE CONTINUOUS (*after* because) *for*
an UNFINISHED ACTION *in the Future*.

Method The teacher gives the stimulus, which the students repeat, adding *because* and the cue provided with the verb in the Future Continuous.

Example

TEACHER: I shan't be able to watch the programme.   do my homework

STUDENT: I shan't be able to watch the programme because I'll be doing my homework.

●*Drill*

I can't telephone him at one o'clock.	have my lunch
The headmaster can't see you then.	teach
She can't come and see you at six o'clock.	put the children to bed
I can't go out with you tomorrow evening.	write an essay
She can't come to the beach with us on Thursday.	take an exam

I shan't be able to see you next week.	work in (Oxford)
She won't be able to attend the meeting tomorrow.	visit her sick brother
I shan't be able to meet you at the station.	have a lesson
We shan't be able to invite them round next week.	decorate the flat
She won't be able to get to the party.	baby-sit
He won't be able to answer the phone.	rest
I can't come out tonight.	listen to the concert
She won't be able to come to the wedding.	stay in Scotland
I shan't be able to hear the bell.	garden
I can't lend you that record tonight.	play it
He can't watch the programme tomorrow night.	attend a meeting
He won't be able to join them for dinner tonight.	study for his exam
She won't be able to recognize him.	he/wear dark glasses
You can't borrow the car tomorrow evening.	I/use it
We can't go bathing at three o'clock tomorrow.	the tide/go out
We shan't be able to stay in tomorrow.	Mary/practise the violin
I can't drive you to the airport tomorrow.	Roger/use the car
We can't look round the cathedral this afternoon.	the choir/practise
You won't be able to make a noise tonight.	the baby/sleep upstairs
We shan't be able to use this room romorrow.	the workmen/decorate it

---

UNIT **109**   *Intermediate*

To practise the FUTURE CONTINUOUS *for a* SECOND, MORE

REMOTE ARRANGEMENT.

Method   The teacher provides the stimulus, which the students repeat, adding *and then* . . . or *and later* . . . followed by a verb in the Future Continuous, as in the example. (In the first ten sentences the students use the same verb as in the stimulus, followed by the cue; in the remaining sentences the cue includes the verb to be used.)

Example
TEACHER: After the meal we're having coffee, . . .　liqueurs
STUDENT: After the meal we're having coffee, and
then/later we'll be having liqueurs.

●*Drill*

He's studying for the Lower Certificate first, . . .	Proficiency
They're playing a Beethoven Overture, . . .	a Mozart Symphony
The team are playing against Italy, . . .	Spain
We're reading Book 2 next week, . . .	Book 3
She's ironing the shirts first, . . .	the handkerchiefs
They're painting the ground floor next week, . . .	the first floor
We're having roast duck and green peas, . . .	ice-cream
He's speaking on television first, . . .	the radio
I'm taking her to the museum in the morning, . . .	the waxworks
We're going to (Nice) for the first week of our holiday, . . .	(Monte Carlo)

We're travelling to (Paris), . . .	go on to (Rome)
We're meeting them at six o'clock, . . .	have dinner together
We're having breakfast early, . . .	go out for the day
I'm taking her to (Westminster Abbey) in the morning, . . .	visit the zoo
He's meeting me at the station, . . .	join the others
She's going to do her homework first, . . .	watch the television
We're painting the outside of the house in the spring, . . .	do up the inside
He's studying Biology first, . . .	take up Anatomy
They're having a big sale soon, . . .	close down
He's showing his paintings in London for a week, . . .	exhibit them in New York
They're modernising the Town Hall first, . . .	rebuild the library
He's leaving school in July, . . .	go to university
She's finishing her training soon, . . .	take a job
She's performing in London next week, . . .	sing in Rome
He's going to study for three more months, . . .	sit for an exam

UNIT 110	*Intermediate*

To practise the FUTURE CONTINUOUS to express a
NORMAL COURSE OF EVENTS.

Method In the first drill, the teacher gives the stimulus, requiring the students to respond with *Don't worry*, . . . and the appropriate cue with the verb in the Future Continuous. In the second drill, he says the first part of the sentence, requiring the students to repeat it and continue with *so* . . . and the appropriate cue with the verb in the Future Continuous negative.

Example
TEACHER: I wonder if he knows about it.   ring him up later
STUDENT: Don't worry, I'll be ringing him up later

● *Drill*

I must tell John about the party.	see him soon
I've forgotten to post this letter.	pass a pillar-box
I want to get some tickets for the theatre.	go into town tomorrow
I don't want to walk home after the party.	bring my car
Your hair's getting terribly long.	get it cut on Monday
I wonder if she's heard the news.	write to her next week
Your watch doesn't keep very good time.	but a new one soon
Are you sure you can afford it?	get a rise soon
Oh dear! I've spilt some coffee on your carpet.	have it cleaned soon
Shall I send the goods up, Madam?	pass the shop tomorrow
Your car looks filthy.	clean it tomorrow
You're looking terribly tired.	get a holiday soon
Shall I cut you some sandwiches?	have lunch on the train
You can't possibly have a party in this room.	get it decorated soon
I haven't got it ready for you yet.	come in again on Thursday

Example
TEACHER: She's moved to (London).   see her again
STUDENT: She's moved to (London), so I shan't be seeing her again.

● *Drill*

Tomorrow's my day on duty, . . .	come home for lunch
I'm going to (the South of France) next week, . . .	teach you
My car's going in for service next week, . . .	drive to work
There's a printing strike, . . .	get any papers tomorrow
Poor Michael's broken his leg, . . .	play football tomorrow
The gramophone's broken, . . .	play records tonight
There's very little work at the office, . . .	work late
She's ill, . . .	sing at the concert
Tomorrow's Saturday, . . .	get up early
He missed a lot of lessons, . . .	take the exam

UNIT **III**   *Intermediate*

To contrast the use of the FUTURE CONTINUOUS *for a*

POLITE QUESTION *with the use of* Will you . . .? *for a*

REQUEST.

Method   First the teacher asks the students to change the orders he gives
them into requests, as in the first example. Having gone through the drill
in this way, he then asks them to turn the same orders into polite questions, as in the second example.

Example 1
TEACHER: Come to see me soon.
STUDENT: Will you come to see me soon (please)?

Example 2
TEACHER: Come to see me soon.
STUDENT: Will you be coming to see me soon?

●*Drill*
Do the washing tomorrow.
Give us a dictation.
Make all the arrangements.
Write to her again.
Play that record this evening.
Do it again.
Go to the Post Office after lunch.
Light a fire in the sitting room.
Make a cake for tea.
Discuss it with her.
Get up early tomorrow.
Take the dog for a walk.
Use this one.
Stay in this evening.
Do your homework before tea.
Buy the tickets.
Meet him at the station.
Sing at the next concert.
Catch the ten o'clock train.
Mow the lawn.

UNIT **112** *Intermediate*

To practise the FUTURE CONTINUOUS *for* EXTRA

POLITENESS.

Example
TEACHER: Are you going to stay in a hotel?
STUDENT: Will you be staying in a hotel?

●*Drill*
Are you going to stay here long?
Are you going to pay for it now?
Are you going to want anything else?
Are you going to visit Mary again this week?
Are you going to need me any more tonight?
Are you going to wear your new suit to the party?
Are you going to go shopping this afternoon?
Are you going to spend much more time here?
Are you going to have anything else to eat?
Are you going to come by car?

How much money are you going to take with you?
Why are you going to leave so early?
When are you going to have the house painted?
What train are you going to catch?
When are you going to have your next lesson?
Where are you going to stay in Paris?
What are you going to have for breakfast?
What time are you going to get back?
When are you going to buy some new shoes?
How many people are you going to invite to the party?
When are you going to take your exam?
What are you going to give him for his birthday?
What time are you going to arrive?
What kind of car are you going to get?
Where are you going to spend the weekend?

UNIT 113 *Intermediate*

To practise the FUTURE CONTINUOUS *used for an*

ASSUMPTION ABOUT THE FUTURE.

Example

TEACHER: I expect it'll get dark soon.
STUDENT: It'll be getting dark soon.

● *Drill*

I expect I'll feel better soon.
I suppose the roses will come out soon.
I reckon the plane will land in a minute.
I think the guests will arrive soon.
I feel sure it'll need a new battery soon.
I bet John will work on Saturday.
I suppose we'll arrive in (Bournemouth) in a minute.
I should think we'll have an election soon.
I bet the fares will go up soon.
I feel certain he'll change his job soon.
I expect they'll get married soon.
I reckon she'll look for a new flat soon.
I expect they'll go to a dance on New Year's Eve.
I bet he'll get the sack soon.
I should think the street lights will go on in a minute.

Example

TEACHER: I don't think they'll take the car.
STUDENT: They won't be taking the car.

● *Drill*

I shouldn't think she'll take the exam.
I don't suppose he'll continue his lessons much longer.
I don't reckon John will come to the party.
I shouldn't think he'll buy her a very expensive present.
I don't suppose he'll use the car this evening.
I shouldn't think they'll arrive before midnight.
I don't suppose she'll stay in (England) much longer.
I shouldn't think they'll go on holiday this year.
I don't think David will go to the meeting.
I don't reckon they'll get up early tomorrow.

UNIT **114**   *Intermediate*

To practise the FUTURE CONTINUOUS *used for an*

ASSUMPTION ABOUT THE PRESENT.

Example
TEACHER: I should think he's getting out of the train now.
STUDENT: He'll be getting out of the train now.

●*Drill*
I bet it's raining in (Manchester) now.
I reckon he's just leaving work now.
I expect she's going to bed now.
I should think it's snowing in the mountains now.
I expect she's putting the children to bed now.
I should think Farmer Williams is working in the fields now.
I bet John and Peter are having a wonderful time in (Morocco) now.
I expect they're watching television now.
I should think they're crossing the frontier now.
I reckon she's doing the housework now.
I expect they're taking their exam now.
I should think Mrs Bradley is cooking the lunch now.
I bet Geoff's playing football now.
I expect he's gardening now.
I should think the ship's coming into harbour now.

Example
TEACHER: It's six o'clock. I don't think he's working now.
STUDENT: It's six o'clock. He won't be working now.

●*Drill*
It's half past eight. I shouldn't think they're having dinner now.
It's seven o'clock. I don't suppose he's teaching now.
It's nearly lunchtime. I shouldn't think she's shopping now.
It's freezing cold. I don't suppose they're sitting in the garden now.
It's eleven o'clock. I shouldn't think he's doing his homework now.
It's raining. I shouldn't think they're playing tennis now.
It's half past six. I don't suppose they're sunbathing now.
It's very late. I shouldn't think he's listening to the radio now.
It's raining. I don't think he's cleaning the car now.
It's midnight. I shouldn't think she's having a bath now.

THE FUTURE PERFECT SIMPLE

To introduce the FUTURE PERFECT SIMPLE *by contrasting*

it with the PAST PERFECT SIMPLE *and the* PRESENT

PERFECT SIMPLE.

Method The teacher says the stimulus and the students repeat it, continuing in the pattern shown in the example. In each response three kinds of change are required in the second and third parts: (i) the adverb of time, e.g. yesterday/now/tomorrow, last month/now/next month; (ii) the tense; (iii) the amount or number, which should increase in a way consistent with the objects and time involved.

Example
TEACHER: Up to yesterday I'd written three letters.
STUDENT: Up to yesterday I'd written three letters, now I've written five letters, and by tomorrow I'll have written ten letters.

●*Drill*
Up to last month he'd saved £100.
Up to yesterday she'd read three chapters.
Up to last week he'd been to that club four times.
Up to last week he'd driven 500 miles.
Up to last week he'd taken her out four times.
Up to yesterday I'd used four gallons of petrol.
Up to last week he'd worn that suit twice.
Up to last week she'd played the record three times.
Up to last year the factory had produced one million cars.
Up to yesterday they'd travelled 200 miles.
Up to yesterday she'd spent £20.
Up to last term he'd taken the exam twice.
Up to yesterday the manager had interviewed three applicants.
Up to yesterday the new doctor had examined five patients.
Up to last year he'd collected 2,000 stamps.
Up to yesterday I'd translated seven pages.
Up to last week they'd built ten houses.
Up to yesterday the surgeon had performed ten operations.
Up to yesterday the chicken had laid four eggs.
Up to yesterday he'd had four driving lessons.

UNIT 116   *Intermediate*

To practise the FUTURE PERFECT SIMPLE *with* by then.

Method In the first drill, the teacher gives the stimulus, and the students respond with 'Yes', using the appropriate cue with the verb in the Future Perfect Simple and *by then*. The same examples are now repeated, the students responding with 'No' and the appropriate cue with the verb in the Future Perfect Simple, negative, and *by then*.

In the second drill (*Example* 3), the teacher gives the stimulus, and the students respond with 'No' and the appropriate cue with the verb in the Future Perfect Simple and *by then*.

Example 1
TEACHER: Can I borrow your bicycle on Saturday?   mend
STUDENT: Yes, I'll have mended it by then.

Example 2
TEACHER: Can I borrow your bicycle on Saturday?
STUDENT: No, I shan't have mended it by then.

● *Drill*

Can you give me your essay tomorrow?	write
Let me know what you think on Monday.	make up my mind
Tell me if you like that record tomorrow.	play
Can you let me have a copy of your book by Christmas?	finish
Let me know the answer on Wednesday.	find out
Couldn't they stay in your spare room at Easter?	decorate
Can you let me have the letter by half past ten?	type
Will you be able to lend us your gramophone for the party?	have it repaired
Can I have your homework in tomorrow?	do
Will you know if he's coming by the weekend?	hear
Let me know what you think of the report on Monday.	read
Can I mention it to him when I see him?	tell
Tell me which you want on Thursday.	decide
Will you be able to go away at the beginning of December?	break up
Shall we come round at eight o'clock?	eat

Example 3

TEACHER: Surely you're not going out tonight in
that dirty old suit.   change

STUDENT: No, I'll have changed by then.

●*Drill*

I hope you won't come to the party with your hair like that.	have it cut
Don't let the guests see those dirty ashtrays when they arrive.	empty them
Are you going to watch that programme at ten o'clock?	go to bed
Are you going round to see them (at Easter)?	move
Shall I ring him up at his office at six o'clock?	leave
Shall I tell her when I see her?	see her myself
She'll go mad when she comes back and sees that beard!	shave it off
Will you still be angry with me on Saturday?	forgive you
I hope you won't have that cold for the party.	get rid of it
Do you want to borrow my car when you're on holiday?	buy one myself
Will it be inconvenient if we come at two o'clock?	have lunch
Will he be here next February?	emigrate
Will he still be at university next autumn?	leave

UNIT **117**   *Intermediate*

To practise the FUTURE PERFECT SIMPLE *with* by

(Saturday).

Method The teacher asks the questions and the students answer in the
pattern shown in the example, using the Future Perfect Simple and
supplying any suitable expression of time (after *by*).

Example

TEACHER: Have they repaired the road yet?

STUDENT: Not yet, but they'll have repaired it by Saturday.

●*Drill*

Have you read that book yet?

Have they got married yet?

Have you written the letter yet?

Have they moved to their new house yet?

Have they paid for their new television yet?

Have you mended the radio yet?
Has she typed the report?
Have you taken your library books back?
Have they had lunch yet?
Have you posted the letters?
Have you collected your gramophone record from the shop?
Have you finished your homework yet?
Have you sent that parcel off yet?
Has she done the washing?
Have you decided yet?
Have you told him yet?
Has she ironed my shirt yet?
Has he cashed the cheque yet?
Have you played the record yet?
Have you made up your mind yet?

UNIT 118   *Intermediate*

To practise the FUTURE PERFECT SIMPLE *for an*

ASSUMPTION ABOUT THE PRESENT.

Method In the first two drills of this unit the students transform the teacher's sentences as shown in *Examples* 1 and 2. The sentences thus formed by the students are then used as responses in the third and fourth drills. Cues are provided, but they should be used only if necessary.

Example 1
TEACHER: I expect he's heard it by now.
STUDENT: He'll have heard it by now.

●*Drill*
I expect he's finished by now.
I'm sure she's read it by now.
I expect the plane has landed by now.
I should think he's written the letter by now.
I expect he's used it by now.

I bet he's worked it out by now.
I should think they've arrived by now.
I expect he's shaved off his beard by now.
I feel sure they've done it by now.
I reckon he's got home by now.
I'm sure he's thought of it by now.
I expect the plane has taken off by now.
I reckon she's left by now.
I should think they've arranged it by now.
I expect he's received it by now.

Example 2
TEACHER: I shouldn't think the train has arrived yet.
STUDENT: The train won't have arrived yet.

●*Drill*
I shouldn't think he's recovered yet.
I don't expect the film has started yet.
I don't reckon he's got there yet.
I'm sure he hasn't looked at them yet.
I don't expect they've gone to bed yet.
I'm sure he hasn't got it yet.
I don't expect they've sent off the goods yet.
I shouldn't think he's seen that film yet?
I'm sure she hasn't put the car away yet.
I don't expect he's read it yet.

Example 3
TEACHER: I'd better telephone him about it, hadn't I?   hear about it
STUDENT: He'll have heard about it by now.

●*Drill*

Wait till he's had lunch.	finish
Shall I lend her a copy of the report?	read
It's six o'clock.	land
I'd better get him to change the letter.	write
Tell him to take it back to the shop.	use
Ring him up and tell him the answer.	work it out
It's half past two already.	arrive
I'd like to see him in a beard.	shave it off
Perhaps they oughtn't to do it after all.	do it
I'll wait a few minutes before I ring him.	get home
Shall I ring him up and remind him?	think of it
We must try and stop him.	take off
I wonder if we can stop her coming.	leave
I think I'll ask them to cancel it.	arrange it
I bet he's impatient to get that letter.	receive it

Example 4
TEACHER: We'd better hurry.   arrive
STUDENT: The train won't have arrived yet.

●*Drill*

It's rather rude not to invite him to our party.	recover
We haven't got time to buy any sweets.	start
We'd better hurry, otherwise we'll miss him.	get there
I must ask him which photographs he wants.	look at them
You'd better not ring them up now.	go to bed
I'm expecting him to ring up about the letter I wrote him.	get it
It's too late to cancel the order.	send off the goods
We can't ask him to come with us.	see that film
We can't very well ask her to take us home.	put the car away
I must ask him what he thinks of that book.	read it

THE FUTURE PERFECT CONTINUOUS

To introduce the FUTURE PERFECT CONTINUOUS *by*

contrasting it with the PAST PERFECT CONTINUOUS *and*

the PRESENT PERFECT CONTINUOUS.

Method The students repeat the stimulus and continue as in the example, changing the time and tense and adding one to the number of years (days, hours, etc.).

Example
TEACHER: Last year I'd been living in . . . for five years.
STUDENT: Last year I'd been living in . . . for five years, now I've been living in . . . for six years, and by next year I'll have been living in . . . for seven years.

Note In the sentences marked *, the teacher should give a time one hour before the drill is being practised.

●*Drill*
Last year he'd been studying English for three years.
Yesterday she'd been staying here for three days.
Last year he'd been learning to play the piano for six years.
*At . . . o'clock he'd been sleeping for three hours.
*At . . . o'clock he'd been standing there for an hour.
Last month he'd been working in that factory for six months.
*At . . . o'clock they'd been watching television for two hours.
Last week she'd been knitting that pullover for four weeks.
Yesterday he'd been waiting for that letter for two days.
Last month she'd been lying in hospital for four months.
Yesterday he'd been wearing that shirt for four days.
*At . . . o'clock they'd been playing tennis for an hour.

The following habitual ideas may be practised in the same way.

Last month he'd been taking her out for four months.
Last year she'd been going to that dentist for eight years.
Last year he'd been travelling up to town every year for thirteen years.
Last week he'd been writing her a letter every week for six weeks.
Last year she'd been catching the 7.30 train every morning for ten years.

UNIT **120**   *Intermediate*

To practise the FUTURE PERFECT CONTINUOUS *with*

by then.

Method   The teacher gives the stimulus, requiring the students to respond with *By then* and the appropriate cue with the verb in the Future Perfect Continuous, followed by a suitable time phrase with *for*.

Example
TEACHER: He's going back to America on Saturday.   stay here
STUDENT: By then he'll have been staying here for six months.

● *Drill*

She's taking her exam in December.	study
They're getting engaged at Christmas.	go out together
He's not stopping work until eight o'clock tonight.	work
He's giving up work next year.	mend watches
The band won't be able to go home till after midnight.	play
According to the forecast, this rain's going on till Saturday.	rain
That play's coming off in August.	run
She's retiring next year.	teach
He won't get home till ten o'clock.	drive
They're moving to a new house at the end of the year.	live here
He says he won't finish his homework till seven o'clock.	write
She's taking her driving test next week.	have lessons
The doctor says he can't get up till Sunday.	lie in bed
The gardener's stopping work at half past five.	dig
I shall finish this book by Saturday.	read it
She's going on holiday in August.	save up
She's coming out of the nursing home on Monday.	convalesce
The meeting won't be over before lunch-time.	go on
He'll be ready for the big race on Saturday.	train